Green Paddler

Paula Johanson

Published by Doublejoy Books, 2022.

GREEN PADDLER

First edition. September 23, 2022.

ISBN: 978-1989966242

Written by Paula Johanson.

Remembering Marlene

Introduction

Most of what I've written about paddling was during the years my spouse Bernie and I lived right next to the finest beach in Victoria.

There are many candidates for 'the finest beach in Victoria' but Cadboro Bay scores high on several scales. There is a bay, offering some shelter from wind, which is important when the usual weather report includes a Small Craft Warning. The shorelines rise on both sides, and within the curve a motorboat can fill the bay with its roar. There's a couple of rock gardens to play in, and several charming little islands are temptingly near. The bay is also sheltered from tidal currents that whirl past this end of the island, currents so fast and strong we call the one near shore The Freight Train. The bay has a beach, and a sandy beach at that. Along part of the beach is a raised promenade, for people with mobility challenges, and a playground of large concrete animals for challenging the mobility of anyone willing to clamber like a child. In Cadboro Gyro park's low, grassy field are a few benches and picnic tables, damp in frequent rains. The public restrooms are large, well-built, and cleaned regularly. A tap offers water! From the gravel parking lot, there's a sandy slope for bringing a kayak, canoe, dinghy, or paddleboard to water. Two bus stops are a quiet block away, at a small grocery store, two coffee shops, and a pub. In short, everything a paddler needs is here, and one of the coffee shops has WIFI.

Sungayaka was what the Songhees First Nations called the bay, for patches of snow. It's where they hunted ducks from small boats at night with torches. There were two small villages on the shore in 1842 when the Hudson Bay Company schooner *Cadborough* anchored here. One village, Chekonein, was at one end of a sandy beach so wide and broad at low tide that First Nations people would play qonwallis, a kind of shinny or lacrosse. The other village was on a little point of land within the bay that became, of course, the Royal Victoria Yacht Club.

Now there are houses all around the bay, but you can only see part of any house, and little of many of them, because there are so many trees here. There are more trees around the bay than there are masts for the boats tied up at the Yacht Club with their rigging ringing like little bells in the breeze off the water. There are more trees than there are houses. Hey, there are more trees than there are windows, even when a cruise ship glides past in the evening with every window lit. In the morning on a clear day, it's possible to see two volcanoes from a boat in the mouth of the bay, and three mountain ranges, to the south, east, and north-east.

The first house next to the park is almost hidden under a willow tree. It's owned by the mother of a friend from our days at university. My partner and I rented a room there, sharing the kitchen and bath with our friend's mother. She was away for days at a time, so we looked after her dogs. The porch beside our door held our kayaks and bikes. We could get up from our hand-me-down desks and chairs, pick up a kayak, and walk two hundred yards to the water. And did so, at any time of day and in all kinds of weather.

The first kayak we bought was second-hand from a rental place on Beaver & Elk Lake, a short and wide recreational boat called a Pamlico. We took turns paddling, but it soon became clear when paddling with friends that we'd need another kayak so we could both go out at the same time. I collected enough pop bottles to buy a folding inflatable kayak on deep discount, one that had been a display model in a marine supply store. Later, I bought an Eliza sea kayak from the rental fleet at a paddle store, and Bernie built his own sea kayak. The makers of my folding inflatable were so happy with what I wrote about it on our paddling group's website Kayak Yak, that over the next few years they gave me three more models to try. We had a fleet of seven boats, but no couch and rarely a vehicle outside our little home.

Soon after we moved into our room in the house under the willow tree, we started calling it the Beach House. With our grown kids working a province away, we needed only space to write and sleep. We knew it was modest, but a good place to live, the first day we walked there from my parents' house after planning their move to a condo. We walked through the university campus, stopping at the library, then on to Sinclair hill that runs down to Cadboro Bay.

It was a sunny day, with the bay shining blue as any calendar photo, and a few little yachts and sloops out sailing with their bright sails and spinnakers.

Trees along the park paths were silhouetted against the blue water, and the little islands looked close enough to reach out and touch.

"Look!" my partner gasped. "*That's where we live!*"

There are inherent risks in paddling any kind of small boats. This author has tried to describe hazards. Changing conditions of weather, tide, and more can challenge paddlers in unexpected ways. It is up to each person to learn the skills needed for safe paddling, including how to be cautious. Even familiar waters are inherently dangerous. In some places, like my home waters, safe conditions can change completely in a few minutes. Paddlers reading this book should have in-person lessons from experienced advisors. The author and publisher disclaim any liability for injury or other damage a reader might sustain.

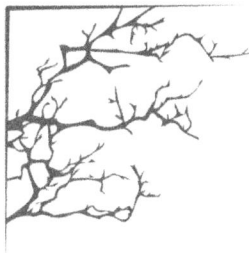

Home Waters

A fabulous day on the water, once again. We seem to have a lot of them. But then, get on the water in small boats on a bunch of days and odds are, some of the days will be fabulous.

This day the tide and currents conspired to make possible a crossing to the Chathams and Discovery Island. The weather was on our side, too! Sunny without being too hot, a slight breeze but not enough to keep us from going.

We set out at nine this morning, and kept closer to the shore of Cadboro Bay than we might have. The middle of the bay had several little sail boats, and it's good to give them lots of room. Yacht owners and power boaters have a special nickname for kayaks: speedbumps. There's even an approved safety tip for what to do when being run over by a powerboat or yacht... as it's about to hit your kayak, roll over, away from the approaching boat. The bigger, faster boat will strike your hull instead of your head. Possibly it will cut your kayak in half, but at least it's apparently less likely to hurt you. I'm not anxious to try the technique. We try to stay out of the way of bigger boats.

Along the shore, John spotted an animal running along the rocks. It was too quick to be photographed, and too small for a river otter. It looked like a mink to me... or maybe a very young otter. Quick as a wink!

The crossing went well. At Chatham and Strongtide, there was just a bit of swirling eddy from the slight flood tide. We wandered around Chatham and checked out the long inlet to see if we could reach the little islet that Rich and Mike Jackson call Cactus Island.

Nope! There wasn't enough water to get in to the basin still surrounding the islet. We landed and walked up the gravel, past the trickle of water still flowing out, to look around. Crossing the trickle of water was a row of rocks like a little dam about ankle-high, reminding me of the rock walls made in the past by First Nations as a fish weir or clam bed. This one could have been just a little dam made by someone playing, but still, nice to see.

5

Out the little inlet, past kingfishers. around rocks and viewing eagles. John got some terrific photos! I'll leave the great story of the eagle meal to him to tell.

We ended up going around Discovery – the mild weather made this a great day. At the campground we took a moment to check out a boat that brought a load of tourists to the park. Looks like a fun idea, but we were very glad to be able to take our own boats out under our own power on this wonderful day.

On the way back, we passed Jemmy Jones Island and Flower. Otters were out again, diving near Flower. Just one more beautiful thing to see! A great trip and still great when we got back to shore. I got back to the Beach House just in time for the lunch Bernie made, and then to Olive Olio's to meet John & Louise, who had found Rich and his Mom. They had come to the Cadboro Bay village on their Vespa-style scooters to meet us after paddling. (Yes, Victoria is the kind of place where a guy just might go zooming around on a scooter with his mom!) Great day, great friends.

TWO VOLCANO DAY!

It's so nice to have a two volcano day on the water, when both volcanoes are conveniently visible in the cloudy weather. Rainier peeked in and out of the low cloud as I was paddling away from the beach at Gyro Park, so I went out around Flower Island and edged over to Evans Rock to see if Baker was visible as well. Yup, Baker was shouldering aside clouds out its way.

Amazing to live in such a beautiful place, with wonders like this accessible in my kayak. As well as big wonders, there were small ones here too: merganser ducks and surf scoters flying, little Mama Seal nosing up to look at me before dipping down, and the astonishingly clear water. Sadly, there are no visible starfish crawling around where I can see them right now.

It's convenient living near a few dormant volcanoes. There are others along the coast, and some emit steam and vapours from time to time, but we don't seem likely to have another big blast like Mount Saint Helens did in 1980 down in Oregon. I wouldn't mind a little eruption, though – just enough to remind the city planners in Vancouver, Victoria, and Seattle that we in big cities really gotta plan what to do when the environment shakes things up. Our padding friend Rich used to say that he figured he'd be on the water when the big earthquake comes or a volcano erupts, and he would ride the wave.

YEP, IT'S FEBRUARY all over. Even the sunny days are pretty chill. So on Saturday the 21st, when Richard and I went paddling, I just had a short trip while he did a second, longer loop before going back to shore.

Launching at Gyro Park is easy for me, with the wheels to roll my Eliza from the house down to the water. Lucky for me, Rich was willing to meet me there instead of at a new beach, and lately, he's been ready at a moment's notice to go kayaking because he's been keeping his boat on the roof of his van.

The tide was just ebbing from high, so there was no current to speak of. Out we went, past Flower and over to look at Cadboro Point. There was a bit of a breeze over the calm water that picked up as we got closer to the point, and through the gaps in the rock we could see chop and whitecaps on the other side. Amazing how one side of a point will have such different conditions from the other side...

Turning around, we went towards Jemmy Jones Island until the chop got me unsettled. Back towards Flower Island, then, no seals or otters in sight, though I saw both earlier that week. That's where we split up, so I could get back to shore before getting chilled and Richard could do another loop and get a good workout.

It was a good moment to get back to the beach, by the way – we saw my neighbour who gets on the water 200 days a year, in his kayak or on his paddleboard. The evening before, Friday, he'd been on the paddleboard out by the Chathams and surprised a male Stellar's sea lion. "Yep, the heart monitor was showing my heart rate at a steady 120 beats per minute until I saw him," he reported. "Then it spiked up to 170." No kidding – bull sea lions are 18 to 20 feet long! Now he was on his way in his kayak with a camera to see if he could get a picture. What a man, what a man...

After Rich got back to shore, there was coffee, there was hot cocoa and hummus at Olive Olio's, there was sundry scanning of Volume one of the *BC*

Atlas for Coastal Recreation Kayaking and Small Boats and various plans for attending Ladysmith's Paddlefest and doing some day trips around Nanaimo, but that was all after the fact. Getting on the water was what mattered, out under the bright blue-and-white bowl of the sky.

ORDINARY WINTER DAY

Another ordinary winter day here. Walked the landlady's dogs and realized that it was not windy, not raining, and not 5 minutes before we had to be someplace else. Quick pot of porridge for both of us. Got into the shortie wetsuit and carried the Mini-Tripper kayak down to the shore. A leaden grey sky as the sun was rising promised me that rain and wind would soon be here.

Today's OK message from my SPOT device was sent from the beach at Gyro Park. I did go farther than that, honestly. But as I walked down the boat ramp, a sweet old lady engaged me in conversation. She seemed really concerned that I had a proper grasp of safety.

As regularly happens, my tow rope, throw bag of floating rope, waterpump, and PFD were all inspected. (My paddle float was with the other set of safety gear for my darling Eliza sea kayak – no need for a paddle float with this little rec kayak.) The design and merits of the kayak were discussed and compared with other boats; not, I hasten to add, because my inspector had any expertise in the matter, but because she wished to be reassured about my own experience and competence.

The last thing I want during these outings is to have fussing shorewalkers panicking and calling 911. Well, okay, the last thing I want is to drown a hundred feet offshore while five dogwalkers try to call 911 on their cellphones (and cuss if there's no signal) and a couple of horrified ancient onlookers have heart attacks or strokes watching me. A close second is not drowning, but flailing my way ashore only to press the Emergency button on my SPOT for the heart attack victims. So I guess not wanting people to make an unneeded emergency call comes third on my list of Things I Really Don't Want To Happen While Kayaking.

The first item that Bernie expected would be on that list – No Spiders Crawling On Me! – already happened once, between Flower Island and Jemmy Jones Island. Louise reported that she was wondering why I'd popped my boat's skirt and was scrabbling around inside the Eliza. It looked like I was having an epileptic seizure. Then she heard me babbling, "Out! Everybody out! You are not my spider friend! You can swim for all I care!" At least, that's the babble that's repeatable in polite company.

All the other spiders are my spider friends, as far as I'm concerned, like the big one who rode along with Bernie and me on my first crossing of Baynes Channel to the Chathams, on a cold January morning. That morning, Bernie walked to the shore, and rushed back to the Beach House to tell me that the water was like glass. It was a perfect day for me to cross the channel with him. It wasn't until we were done with our kayaks back in the yard and I was tidying the gear that this particular spider crawled out from under the seat of my Eliza kayak, shivering, and asked "Are we done yet?" I was so grateful that the big hairy spider had not crawled on me when we were half-way across the channel, that I carefully picked it up with two sticks (BIG spider, eh?) and put it in the garden. Good spider. My spider friend. *shudder*

Ahem.

As for this morning, it took some conversation to show the concerned passer-by that she didn't have to engage the help of a couple of joggers to save me from a reckless expedition. When she asked if I had a way to contact people, I showed her the SPOT beacon and pressed the OK button.

Eventually she went on her way, much less concerned. I paddled along to the little rock garden and began doing a figure eight around the rocks. Just then, a river otter popped up and down several times. He swam to the largest rock and climbed ashore with something in his mouth, maybe a fish or a crab. Clearly it was something tasty, as he began tearing off mouthfuls. He looked in my direction after a few moments, so I quickly averted my face. (I think animals feel more threatened when we look directly at them. Sometimes they don't mind if I peek once in a while with a sidelong glance out of the corner of my eye.)

Apparently it was breakfast time for the otter here, and not my turn in the rock garden. I kept rocks between us and beat a hasty retreat back to the shore. The breeze was just starting to pick up.

A few raindrops fell as I put the kayak away. Some teenagers on a bottle drive came up the driveway and asked if we had any empty bottles. So I plodded across the wet yard with some of ours. The puddle in the front yard is colder than the ocean this time of year. But at least it washed the sand out of my sandals.

It's a rainy, breezy morning now, just right for using my computer. I'm tucked under my years-old sleeping bag, editing the page proofs of my next book.

PADDLEFEST AND THE Least Lonely Solo Paddle

Good times were had in Ladysmith at Paddlefest. One year, Bernie and I rode the train with our little knapsacks and a folding inflatable kayak, and got off at Ladysmith station right next to Transit Beach. We rolled our gear along and met our friends already having a great time. John wrote about Day One of the festival on Kayak Yak blog. He and Louise gave Marlene a ride up to Ladysmith, and got recognized by a couple from Medicine Hat who read Kayak Yak. Nice to meet fellow enthusiasts!

Glad to see Tracey at Paddlefest, too, on her way back from getting her kayak repaired in Comox. I think she left while a number of us were trying out some kayaks on the beach and Bernie was setting up the tent.

The couple from Medicine Hat recognized Bernie too, a couple hours later at a picnic bench. More good conversation! We ended up sharing a couple of bags of those tiny donuts with them and Marlene, John, and Louise, fresh-made donuts from a vendor's booth. Hint: ask the vendor to go easy on the sugar & cinnamon that she shakes into the bag. We were happy with 1/3 the usual amount.

Then it was time to do a workshop discussion on inflatable kayaks. John took photos of me showing and discussing my Advanced Elements Dragonfly (the older version of their new Lagoon) and a couple of borrowed boats. Ocean River Sports kindly loaned me the Aeris Sport for the workshop, and it got poked & prodded and its design studied. The sales rep from Necky Kayaks and Alberni Outfitters also were kind enough to loan me their Advanced Elements

AirFusion for the workshop. This is a sweet design, and very different from most inflatables! I was glad to review this model for Kayak Yak.

The ultimate thing to say about inflatable kayaks, is that there's no one perfect boat. Each paddler has her or his own goals, place, strength, and interests to consider. Not everyone is a commando kayaker like Dubside, who writes about his experiences paddling and as a guide. He prides himself on being able to carry his boat and gear easily into odd or distant places like commandos did during World War II. We met at a Paddlefest one summer, while he was demonstrating rolling techniques. For me also, portable and light is the most important feature, so I use a small kayak that is also stable because of my balance issues. For a fisherman, other choices would work better. Bernie's comments on kayak selection seemed to be more on target for the participants, new to inflatable kayaks.

After the workshop, Bernie and I walked up into town, and walked around. We decided to eat a pizza from a funky artsy place on Roberts Street, just half a block up and across the highway from the exit to Transfer Beach. Good choice! Good pizza made on the spot by friendly youths with good ingredients.

After dinner, we went to sleep. Yeah, yeah, old people. Hey, we'd been up since five am, hauled two big bags of inflatable kayaks and two knapsacks of camping gear onto the train and down to the beach, and been busy all day. But yes, apparently we are old because we slept for ten hours. Pleased to say that neither of us was zoolander'd (can't turn left) by any crick in the neck.

We walked up the hill into town for breakfast with a nice couple from Nimbus Kayaks. Then back to get at our plans for the morning! Bernie set off on a four-hour hike, training for his big expedition in June. He went around some trails shown on a sign at Transfer Beach, and came back tired and sore with good photographs.

I set up my Dragonfly and launched it at Transfer Beach. The weather was good – a high, bright overcast with almost no breeze. The plume from the Crofton mill was rising straight up. Over the next three hours, I did a very enjoyable figure eight in Ladysmith Harbour. First I went around Wood Island (the smaller, southern of the two under this name on the map in John Kimatas's *BC Atlas Volume One*), then around the Dunsmuir Islands.

At the little Wood Island I was careful to avoid log booms (floating rafts of logs) tied up around it and the bigger Wood Island. It's not that an accident with the logs is all that likely, it's just that when a log rolls on top of a kayaker, he or she is so *very* thoroughly drowned that it's all over but the inquest. It was great to see the sandstone galleries and lace rock all along this narrow little island. John took this photo last year at this spot.

At the northern tip of this little island is a sign advising that one is now at the 49th parallel of latitude. I clicked the OK button on my SPOT here. You can see the place on a Google map, and I recommend zooming in and clicking on the Satellite option to see the islands, which don't show on the street map.

A good spot to pause and think a while about the world, while staying carefully away from the log booms. And while pausing there, I met another white-haired woman kayaker, Bev. And Bev recognized me from the Kayak Yak blog. aaAAaa! We chatted awhile and plan to meet to paddle together this summer. Then we went on our way, and as Bev had advised me, there were indeed eagles and raccoons to see on and around the Dunsmuir Islands.

These rocky little islands are connected at low tide, and the tide was indeed low that morning. The water is very shallow around Dunsmuir, and I was pleased to see eelgrass growing in the sandy bottom. Many small red crabs were walking sideways through the eelgrass, among a few clamshells and also the egg cases for Moon snails. On the flats exposed to the bright hazy day, from time to time a squirt of water would shoot up, so there must be big clams like geoducks in that sand. There were certainly shell beaches and middens all over that part of the harbour!

I had a blast paddling alone in Ladysmith Harbour, but then, this wasn't the first time I visited and we did explore the little islands of Wood and Dunsmuir pretty thoroughly last summer. I wouldn't recommend someone taking so little a boat as my Dragonfly here alone on their first outing on a windy day, but I've had the Dragonfly out in all kinds of weather and places over the last four years. There was barely any breeze and there was very little powerboat traffic to avoid when crossing from or to Transfer Beach. What with all the kayaks from Paddlefest, the herons I passed going and coming, the powerboats with their carefully genteel wakes, and an abundance of wildlife of many kinds, this was the least lonely solo paddle I've had in ages.

IT'S ALWAYS A PLEASURE to bring a kayak to Beaver Lake or Elk Lake. This kind-of hourglass shaped lake is a sheltered place to paddle, and it's pretty popular in summer. That makes it a good winter paddle for our group. The other times I come here is on days that I'm volunteering as a naturalist in the Nature Centre. It's nice to show up early with a little inflatable and spend an hour noodling around the lake before opening the Nature Centre.

Today I saw more boats on the lake than ducks – and that counts the mallard with her nine fuzzy baby ducklings. There were sit-on-top kayaks, Pelicans, a couple of canoes, and some short recreational kayaks, all buzzing around the lake. Most fun of all was seeing a truck in the parking lot with the back full of boat – two short rec kayaks pointing backwards and one sea kayak pointing forward to the sky over the truck cab.

So it was definitely summer at Beaver Lake: lots of boats, people picnicking, and other people running through the beach area on the jogging trail. Also, the water was green with a bit of an algae bloom.

Before going on the lake, I sent a SPOT OK message while talking about my gear with a jogger. It was a good day! And the Nature Centre has a new exhibit... a river otter, stuffed and mounted. Nice to get a close-up look at an otter.

TOOK SOME TIME ONE Sunday morning to go kayaking with John and Louise, into a fogbank thick as pea soup. We went from Cadboro Bay past Cattle Point to Mary Tod Island and back, a trip we've done a dozen times before. In the fog, it was a trip into mystery. I don't think we got more than a hundred yards offshore, except for a few minutes in Oak Bay when we took compass bearings and turned round at Mary Tod to face into the mist and away from the dimly-seen shore.

Shall have to put that sense of "anything could be in that fog" into my next fantasy novel. (Meanwhile, my first novel had just been launched!) And after launching our boats, and the short journey, we returned to shore, safe in our home waters with our little compasses pointing the way. Some people dream of going out on the water like this, and we're lucky enough to do it over and over.

WHALE WATCHING

Hey folks! Part of the reason there was no official paddle this weekend was that Bernie and I volunteered with Straitwatch on Saturday.

This is an organization that collects data for the federal government on the whale watching so popular in this area. Bernie and I met Kathy at 8:30 am and got back to shore at 5:40 pm.

Kathy gave us an orientation spiel and then fired up their 18-foot Zodiac. We zoomed over to Discovery Island and hung out for a while, listening to radio reports.

When her counterparts at Soundwatch (the Puget Sound organization that collects data also) reported whale sightings near San Juan Island, we headed off in that direction. It turned out to be more than one whale, or pod. The superpod of J, K and L pods had gotten together for a big family barbecue equivalent. There were eighty to ninety whales, according to Kathy, and we saw several groups of three or more. Some even approached the Zodiac to within 50 metres!

All day, we enjoyed seeing whales and some seals near San Juan Island and Lopez Island. There were usually eight to twelve small vessels nearby, watching whales, and most of the time the international rules about Not Approaching Whales were observed. Good!

I enjoyed seeing unfamiliar beaches, and the opposite side of a very familiar two-humped hill on San Juan Island. The islands looked like the ones we paddle among in Canadian waters... makes me remember that border is an intellectual line, not a physical one. We hadn't expected to cross the border, but the day went well and a good time was had by all as Bernie and I figured out what we were supposed to be doing as volunteers. Bernie did most of the data recording;

I mostly grinned and had a good time. It was like having a personal whale watching tour!

The most confusing moment of all was when a small steel-coloured boat came by, flying an American flag. "That's Homeland Security," said Kathy. We tried not to look like terrorists... but I'm not really sure what they were looking for. Frankly, if whale watching or gathering data on whale watchers is making Homeland Security suspicious, well, we've all got to have some more communication that eases those suspicions.

It took an hour of high-speed travel – much faster than a kayak, the Zodiac has two four-stroke engines that howled their way through over 80 litres of fuel – to get us back to the Oak Bay Marina. Bernie and I saw a hummingbird, and hopped on a bus, then transfered to the bus to the Beach House. Next time we'll bike instead of bussing to the Marina for a great day on the water.

Note to self: sunscreen doesn't stop windburn when roaring along in a Zodiac. Still, no regrets.

Heeeeeere, Whale! Wha-ale!

NOPE, NO VISIBLE WHALE today. And I looked, too!

I headed out along the Uplands shoreline of Cadboro Bay this afternoon, out past Loon Bay and Spurn Head into the Big Rock Garden. That's where all the mansions have manicured lawns and rock walls that run down to the water.

So, there weren't any whales that I saw, but it was great to get out on the water. Any day I get to see two volcanoes (both Mt Baker and Mt Rainier) is a good weather day if nothing else, and a good day for my inner geologist. While I didn't see the whale that our friend Jono saw from Cattle Point last night, there were dozens of semi-aquatic mammals on the beach at Gyro Park. Fashion alert: Bikinis have now become teeny-tiny again. When did that happen? I must have missed the memo. And while the truly marvelous little beaches at the Big Rock Garden were, as almost always, empty, I did manage to catch sight of not just one, but six specimens of the sub-species Rich Human Beings.

Okay, okay, I know that pretty much everyone living in Victoria could be identified in the field guide for Rich Human Beings, but work with me here: some of us are a *little bit more* rich. And whenever we've paddled along this shore, it's rare to see even one person, even on a bright, sunny weekend. This was a mid-week day and I was stunned to see two people in their yards, and two groups of two people descending to the shoreline via public access stairs. Don't ever let anyone tell you that it's a waste of taxpayers' money to build a Public Beach Access. I see 'em getting used. Even in the Uplands, that's how many people get down to the shore and see a bit of what we in our boats get to enjoy so much.

As far as nature goes, I did get to see herons and an oystercatcher, and a couple of otters, and sent another SPOT OK while I was out looking around and smiling.

Maybe I'd have seen the gray whale if I went to Cattle Point... but a breeze was coming up and I had to paddle facing into the breeze all the way back. Not much, really, but it was a reminder to spend only an hour or so on the water, not two or three.

There was enough wind, actually, that the Royal Victoria Yacht Club ad at least two groups of beginners out in little walnut-shell sized boats. Yes, I know that making judgemental comments about the size of a boat is pretty picky for someone who paddles in an 8 1/2 foot inflatable much of the time. I'm just sayin'. Small boats. Shaped like bathtubs. Really.

You can see the RVYC on maps of Victoria, both paper and online maps. From the beach you can usually hear the newbies out in their sailboats for their first or second time. There are few sounds that carry over water better than the sound of a dozen children in a dozen small sailboats... unless it's two dozen children in a dozen small sailboats. There was screeching, and yelping, and several loud smacks.

I ducked inside the breakwater to be out of their way, and out of the breeze for a few yards. It's always nice to see the pretty yachts moored here, and sometimes there's someone cleaning a boat or even taking it out for a spin.

Out among the few sailboats tied up to floats in the bay, I came across Mike Jackson and his friend Dan. They were practising rolls in their Tahe Greenland kayaks... very spiffy looking boats, and so easy to handle. We reminded each other that the municipality of Saanich has Park Plans for Gyro Park, and what the neighbourhood and kayaking community can do to preserve beach access.

Back to shore, and up the sandy ramp while avoiding sunbathers. It wasn't a whale-spotting day, but it was still a good time to be out on the water

ONE THING

Slept in Sunday morning. Hey, winter mornings are dark! And there was a great movie on TV last night – final part of *The Lord of the Rings*. Even with blipping to another channel during the spider attacks, it still kept me awake late. So it was nice to get up a little later than usual.

Pulled my parka on and walked the landlady's dogs. In my neighbourhood it's okay to wear pyjamas while walking dogs, especially if the pjs kinda look like yoga gear instead of being the flannel type with Snoopy dog patterns.

While walking dogs I saw the weather was great for November – cold but no wind or rain. Yay! So you can bet that ten minutes later I was walking through the park again, but this time without dogs and with a rec kayak on my shoulder.

It's been windy too many days lately! We've been making do with kayaking videos instead of going out in the boats. High tide and slack current made it a great day to be on the water.

So nice to go out and do the loop along the beach, along the rocky shore, then out and around Flower Island and back. There were gaps in the cloud cover, and the sun glared down, bright but not hot. It was wonderful to see the water all clear again! In summer, the bay's water grows cloudy. Now, I could even see white sea anemones on the rocks underwater at the rocky shoreline. I turned and swirled, practising some of the extended-reach moves shown in the kayaking videos. Cormorants took off and gave me some room to move.

There were otters tumbling inside the line of bull kelp, so I paddled outside the tangles and managed not to disturb them too. The otters are good neighbours, as far as I can tell. The one that galloped through our front yard this summer was a big friendly fella.

Birds galore floated or flew past. It always amazes me how ducks' wings whistle as they take off or land. Even those little ducky birds called surf scoters. I made note of the black and white wings of one little flock of birds, to look up in bird books.

As I rounded Flower, I went to Evans Rock. Looking one way, there was Mount Rainier, dim but showing through the patchy clouds. Looking another, there was Mount Baker, bright with fresh snow. It was a two-volcano day!

The air was so clean. There wasn't any current in the little channel as I paddled past the rock that looks like a crouching cat. "Just give me one thing I can hold onto/ to believe in..." really gotta learn all the words to that song.

An eagle soared past, and a kingfisher darted by. There's a coffee shop in the neighbourhood, and up high on one of the walls is written:

Hopping out of bed and thinking about the one thing

Then a splash distracted me. The otters were still tumbling inside the line of bull kelp along the shore. I guessed there must still be herring or some other schools of fish gathering in that place. Trying to give them lots of room, I headed farther off-shore, but the otters came up in front of me and ducked down again. One popped up again, close enough that I could see the fish caught in his jaws. Way to go, otter!

Back along the shore, avoiding dogs swimming for tennis balls. Then back to the Beach House with the kayak on my shoulder. Made medlar jelly, and sealed it in mason jars. Wrote and wrote while the wind picked up as the day ended. What a day!

THE INCREDIBLY BIG Bathtub

Sunday, November 4th was a bright morning. When Alison picked me up at Island View Beach at 8:30am, we could see a ring of clouds that boded well for a day of good weather. If we hadn't already set on our plan to paddle from Cadboro Bay around to Island View, this would have been a good day to go to Darcy Island! Probably wouldn't even have been any of the waves that jostled Bernie on his last trip there.

Alison and I left my dad's pickup truck at Island View and drove to Cadboro Bay. I walked from Gyro Park's parking lot all of the few hundred yards to the Beach House, and asked Bernie to carry my Eliza down to the water. After wriggling into my wetsuit, I carried my gear down to the beach, prompting smart-aleck comments about "Carrying it all in one load" from the man who a) carries kayaks solo and b) loads his yellow Chesapeake with four person-loads of camping gear.

The weather was great as we launched between 9am and 9:30, and stayed good all day even as clouds slowly blew in from the south. Alison and I had to hug the shore while leaving Cadboro Bay, to avoid the clouds of small sailboats. Going round Cadboro Point and Ten Mile Point, we were going with the mild current. We even saw our only standing waves of the trip, in a channel by the lighthouse: a series of waves only six inches high. Out in Baynes channel, the freight train was running between the lighthouse and Strongtide Island. Not a good time to make a crossing to Chatham, not till slack around noon. But where we were paddling was as glassy calm as inside Cadboro Bay. Small rollers surfed us northward, but they were only two or three inches high.

The point is longer than Alison figured, and she was surprised to see how far it was to Telegraph Cove. Passing heaps of mansions is always interesting, and rocky cliffs also. The helicopter kept by one fabulously wealthy household was nowhere in sight that day. After Telegraph Cove, we cut across the opening of Finnerty and Arbutus Coves, seeing an eagle on the rocks, then rounded Paul's Terrace with its cluster of new houses, and rounded Gordon Head. At Gordon Rock we saw a seal, possibly the baby that had wanted Louise to take it home for a pet. He looked fine, Louise!

Margaret's Bay was a nice sheltered spot for a bit of lunch and a stretch. The sun was already behind the trees... that's something about this beach and Mount Douglas Park beach, always cool in the shade.

Launching again, Alison borrowed my paddle gloves, but warmed up quickly once we were out in the sun. The water was still glassy calm, so we cut across Cordova Bay, from Cormorant Point almost to the sand bluffs. I checked on the chart, and we were well over a mile off-shore, almost at Little Zero Rock and more than half-way to Zero Rock. The mild current was still assisting us.

Eventually we realized we weren't going to James Island, and changed our angle of approach so we'd come closer to shore near the sand bluffs. Going through the scanty kelp there, we saw that the current had turned and was now drifting against us. Well, we THOUGHT the water had gotten thicker! Still, we were in no rush and just kept paddling with a slower net speed than earlier.

It was a terrific day to be out in a kayak. As long as we were in the sun, we were plenty warm. And the air was cool enough to make wearing proper cool weather gear comfortable.

Just as the sand bluffs seemed to go on forever and Island View beach must have been retreating up to Sidney and so on, Alison said, "Something's sounding." She pointed over towards Darcy, and then I saw what she did.

Two dorsal fins. And two long, black backs.

Several times, these two travellers came up, blew out noisy breaths, and ducked under the water. You know how a seal sounds like a tenor, and a sea lion sounds like a baritone, when they whuff their breath at us? These were bass singers in the ocean choir. Big lungs.

We only saw black backs, no tell-tale white markings of an orca. So we're willing to concede that these may have been Dall's porpoises, closer to us than they looked. But we think they were two minke whales. Maybe. I may have to re-assess harbour seals as sopranos in that ocean choir.

Funny how paddling after that was once again such a cheerful experience, even against a very mild current. We listened to a loon's wild calls, and Alison enjoyed the echoes off the sand bluffs, and eventually we got to Island View beach at 3pm.

So Alison had her 4 hour paddle, which she wants more frequently in training for our planned Red Deer River trip. And I got to see big porpoises at least, if not whales. All in all, a fabulous day.

I GOT OUT TO THETIS Lake last weekend, to meet John and Louise and Alison. It was an expedition with multiple transportation choices. John and Louise took their car with their Delta sea kayaks on top. Alison rode in her own car that's currently being driven by her parents, with her Wilderness Systems Kestrel rec kayak on top. (Shorter than the Deltas, it's a good fit on her smaller sedan. Here's a photo that John took last year at Gyro Park, showing the Kestrel on the sedan.) The Sinclairs waved at their madcap daughter and headed back home to hot tea and scones, I'm guessing, since they had no interest in hanging around the chill beach. I hopped on the bus a block from the Beach House, transferred downtown, and hopped off the jitney (or *le car* in French) at Six Mile House.

Yeah, yeah, so who uses "jitney" for the bus linking a satellite community to an urban core? Or "*le car*" for that matter? Someone who just read an article about Alzheimer's disease, that's who. Apparently people suffering from Alzheimer's who are bilingual can have up to twice as much brain damage as people who show a similar amount of visible signs and symptoms but are not bilingual. In the interest of making my nearly-bilingual brain more resilient in case I'm ever faced with Alzheimer's disease, I'm incorporating vocabulary from French and from other dialects of English into my daily discourse, eh? *D'accord*?

Bilingual observations aside, commando kayaking in winter is less fun than in summer. While it didn't rain during my commute, there were other issues. I arrived at the bus stop ten minutes early for the first run of that Sunday morning, but the bus arrived ten minutes late. So I got downtown too late for the #50 bus and had to wait. Once I finally got to Six Mile House, it's a fair walk over two little hills to the lake. Luckily, a passer-by alerted me when the ball of yarn from my knitting fell out of my pocket. It was unrolling along behind me on the sidewalk, but my knitting hadn't yet begun to unravel – whew!

Meanwhile, John, Louise, and Alison had already arrived at Thetis Lake. They paddled from our usual launch spot at the second beach, around a point and up to the first beach as we arranged. I was not yet there. If you check out John's post on the blog, you can see his drawing of the route he took that morning. It shows that he and Louise and Alison went around in circles for a while, back to a nearby island and back to the beach when they saw me crest the hill and plod down to the beach.

We still had fun. We noodled all over the lake. And it didn't matter a bit whether the wind came up or there were a few raindrops, or more chill than we prefer. The lake is sheltered. That's part of why we paddle lakes in the winter – so we don't have the disappointment of going all the way to an ocean bay that surprises us by being full of rough waves and wind from an unexpected direction.

After paddling, we stuffed my Expedition into the back seat of Louise & John's car and me into the back seat of Alison's sedan (with her parents staring admiringly as the hardshell kayaks were loaded onto the roof racks of both vehicles). Then we retraced my portage from the bus stop to Six Mile House.

Alas, the pub restaurant serves only buffet luncheon until 2pm on Sundays. A fine buffet, but one for people with grand appetites, not those who just wanted soup and tea. So we went our separate ways. I bid goodbye to the rest there, thanking them for saving me the portage, and hot-footed it a long block to the bus stop, where the driver waited for me to trot the last fifty yards to *le car* with my kayak. Yay! *Merci!* Much nicer than waiting 45 minutes for the next scheduled bus to arrive.

The ride and the transfer gave me a chance to knit another few rounds on the latest pair of fingerless mitts for a colleague of Louise's at UVic. Some of us have always felt it's better to wrap the humans up in warm clothes than to turn up the thermostat in winter. These mitts may look like frivolous decorations compared with neoprene kayaking gloves, but I gotta say, if those people in Records and Admissions want to keep warm, I will keep knitting for them!

JAM TART

I have felt like such a jam tart for the last six weeks! As a paddler, anyway.

Louise made me explain that idiom the other day – a jam tart isn't like making REAL tarts with REAL filling from scratch ingredients. Say, sliced fruit glazed with gelatin in baked pastry shells, or lemon meringue tarts or the like. A jam tart is made by spooning a little jam into the pastry shell and baking it. Quick, easy, not the real proper thing. I used to make them as a kid, re-using my mother's pastry scraps so the pastry ended up over-handled and tough too, but kids don't care.

That doesn't sound like it has much to do with kayaking, but bear with me.

Living right by the bay means that I get to see the water every day, and lately I've been jonesing to get out in one of my kayaks. Jonesing every day. What a jam tart I've been, letting a little 'flu and windy cold days keep me from paddling! And I've only been out on the water ... um, six times in the last six weeks.

My partner gently explained that many kayakers get on the water only in the summer, maybe once a week. So maybe I should stop complaining about that and see the doctor about the 'flu.

The doctor listened to my chest and took my temperature, nodded at my achy joints, and prescribed antibiotics for bronchitis. Apparently an opportunistic bacterial infection has moved in after the 'flu softened me up; and before it invites all its little pneumonia buddies to party (hard to evict those little suckers from the *bottom* of the lungs!) I'm supposed to take these mondo antibiotics and kick that infection's ass.

No wonder the 23-pound Dragonfly inflatable felt so goddamned heavy when I carried it at Mill Bay and Nanaimo last week. Wasn't just the addition of a full 1 litre steel water bottle (Louise's gift) and a spare air pump to the usual equipment of paddle, bilge pump and throw bag. It was the little bacteria passenger (!) hanging from my neck saying, "I'm bored, I'm tired, I wanna hot drink and a nap! Aren't you walking the long way around the pavilion?" Good thing I told it: "I'm stoked, I'm limber, I'll sleep when I'm dead! And this IS the short way 'round the pavilion."

(Told Bernie that and he said innocently, "So it wasn't the big weights I put in your bag?" and fled from my bug-eyed glare. If there are horseshoes stuffed in my Dragonfly, there's gonna be a new definition for **commando kayaker** around here.)

So if there aren't daily paddle reports from me about the latest otter sighting or bussing my inflatable across town, well, it's nothing anybody said. I'm just accepting that for the next couple weeks I will be kayaking only on the warmest of days.

WHAT IT TAKES

"What does it take to keep you guys off the water?" one of our friends asked. "You go kayaking on weekends and weekdays. You paddle when it's raining. You paddle in the dark. You paddle in the fog now that you all have compasses. You paddle year-round. You go out in January in a shortie wetsuit and bare feet, for heaven's sake. You guys have been out in wind, snow, ice, and red tides. I've seen some of you out in kayaks even when you have a cold. What does it take to keep you from kayaking?"

Our friend does exaggerate a little. We don't like being out in the wind. And we didn't know about the red tides before we blundered into them (yuck!) at Brentwood Bay. In truth, it doesn't take more than 15 km winds to keep us either off the water or retreating to Thetis Lake and the shelter of its forest park. One year, November and December had nine windstorms that kept us off the water before Christmas. The next year, we took a bit of a break in December, due to a couple of factors.

The first (and most crucial) factor was wind. There was more wind than we like, on many of the weekends. The second factor was temperature. It had been snowing and frosty as well. That's not enough in itself to keep us on land, but with enough wind as well, we've been calculating wind chills often as low as -9 or -18, which is way more than most Islanders usually face.

These two factors even combined are still not enough to keep us on land without the third factor: at least four of us had aches and pains from a mild version of the 'flu. We do NOT want to have the 'flu get any worse!

There are indeed kayakers out in this weather, as I've seen a few convoys of cars with kayaks on top go past me into and out of Cadboro Bay. But I'm guessing those hardcore enthusiasts do not have the 'flu.

It's also worth observing that my partner Bernie and I at last reliably determined what it takes to reduce the numbers of people using Gyro Park in Cadboro Bay at all hours of the day or night. We noticed that a steady stream of people walk in and out of the park all day long, and all night long as well. More people use the park and beach on warm, sunny days, of course. But rain doesn't stop a few people from leaving tracks on the sand. And snow leaves clear traces of just how many people have walked past with a child or dog or little grocery wheeler.

As Bernie puts it, for the park to be empty at night, it takes a temperature below -5 Celsius, with a windchill factor taking it down to -10 or lower, with snow falling on icy roads. Oh, and dark, of course. If it's daylight, there will be at least one hardy soul grimly staring out into the snowfall from the little promenade above the beach.

NOT JUST ANOTHER TRIP Around Flower

Most of the times I'm out in a kayak alone, it's in Cadboro Bay. I salute the Buddha that a neighbour has set up in a rock niche by their little dock, I play in the little rock garden for a while, and I go out to Flower Island, just off the point.

Sunday, May 10, I wasn't out alone ... not at first anyway. I launched with Richard and we found my partner Bernie testing his yellow wooden kayak in Sheep Cove. Meeting as planned, we headed out towards Cadboro Point. The current wasn't yet slack, so the water was moving a little in places. I told the guys to head on where they wanted, and that I'd go back past Flower, taking it easy.

It was a nice time, looking back to see them go to Jemmy Jones and then get blocked from my view by that bald little island. I faced water a little more rough than they did, in the shallows just off Flower where the low tide was making some reefs more obvious in today's version of the currents. Every day, the currents are slightly different and the eddies run wherever they decide to by some arbitrary system. But as Bernie noted on this website in a reply to Alison's post about paddling a Montreal canal, Rich ran with the current and hit 13 or more km/hr!

Not me. I drifted around the rocks near Flower and looked for sea life. Rainbow seaweed and little crab-things were the highlight of that quarter-hour, until suddenly something moved behind my stern.

Splash and howl! I guessed that a seal had come up to slap the water and tell me to get lost. But that was one BIG splash and one LOUD noise. I had my paddle back in the water and was stroking fast to get away by the time I peeked over my shoulder to see that it wasn't a harbour seal, it was a great big sea lion or elephant seal.

Faster! faster! and by this time I was saying out loud, "I'm sorry, you must be a mother, I didn't know you were here, I'm sorry!" And she surfaced again, blew out her breath and roared, honked, and howled at me, over and over again.

I have never been so glad to be in the Eliza, which moves much faster than the little inflatable Dragonfly. Not that either would have been much of an issue for Big Mama to bat aside if she chose. But she didn't, of course; she was instructing me on my bad manners, and stayed a few yards away, splashing her big flipper-feet and rolling up to the surface to roar at me and then duck under again. Rich could hear her noises all the way over at Vantreight Island in the Chathams, but Bernie was sheltered behind Jemmy Jones and didn't hear.

This isn't the first time I've caught a glimpse of of a big sea lion or elephant seal off Flower, but it's the first time that I've ever been noticed by one. My guess is that since the Eliza had been drifting in the shallows for ten or fifteen minutes, that Big Mama didn't know I was a human in a boat and must have been surprised to surface and see that I wasn't some big pink log floating there.

Memo to self: there may be a baby elephant seal or sea lion in that area, so don't get in the way of its mother!

NEW HOME

When we found our new home in Sooke, a town near Victoria, we did so with confidence there were places nearby for paddling that could be reached on foot, or by bus. Here's one good round of commando kayaking among many that summer! I spent time that summer learning all the bus routes in and around Sooke. This time I hopped on the #63 again with my inflatable Lagoon (a dandy little kayak), and hopped off at the sign for Poirier Lake, with two five-car parking lots right beside Otter Point Road. Poirier is a little kidney-bean shaped lake a few hundred metres across, surrounded by tall trees and a hill, with a few houses peeking out from the trees. On the map it looks like the lake drains through a creek into Young Lake nearby. Poirier is one of several small lakes in and near Victoria that are part of a management plan.

As Hook and Bullet website says,

> *Poirier Lake is a lake located just 2.5 miles from Sooke, in Capital Regional District, in the province of British Columbia, Canada. Whether you're fly fishing, baitcasting or spinning your chances of getting a bite here are good. So grab your favorite fly fishing rod and reel, and head out to Poirier Lake. For Fishing License purchase, fishing*

*rules, and fishing regulations please visit Fish & Wildlife website.
Please remember to check with the local Fish and Wildlife department
to ensure the stream is open to the public. Now get out there and fish!*

As a matter of fact, one can go fishing only in lakes or the ocean on the whole island this summer. Long before the Department of Fisheries closed all the streams and rivers due to the dry weather, all the fly-fishing clubs and First Nations had announced that no one should fish in any of the streams or rivers. The poor fish are suffering from low water conditions, with some streams drying up to leave only a few warm pools of water.

I rolled up to the lakeshore and chatted with a pair of workers for Juan de Fuca Recreation and the Capital Regional District. I found the plans for park improvement online. There's a nice picnic shelter here above the shore, and a few picnic tables as well. The paths are crushed gravel, and there is a porta-john. Plans are in place to turn the two concrete pads into the base for good little docks for fishing, one of which will be a boat launch. No motor boats are allowed, but small rowboats, canoes, kayaks and the like are welcome. Swimming is not recommended.

The lake has a shallow muddy bottom on the north-west shore, with at least three kinds of water lilies growing. All around the lake are many sunken logs with branches sticking up near or to the surface. These would be places to look for fishes, and possibly turtles, but neither were visible today.

I turned on my SPOT beacon and sent an OK signal from the lake. Later I sent another OK from the bus stop a little way along the road while I was waiting for the bus. It's a nice way to let Bernie know at home that I've arrived at the lake, and then that I'm waiting at the bus stop after leaving the lake. Paddling alone is less dangerous when a person wears a PFD (always), chooses a sensible place sheltered from strong wind, and has a plan to avoid annoying problems when possible.

I can see why Poirier would be a popular lake for fishing. Not only is it right on a paved road (and a bus route!) but there are clouds of bugs fluttering over the lake so I'm sure the trout are snapping them up. While I was paddling slowly along the south-east shore near the steep hillside, the water looked deeper than where I launched. It was cool in the shade from the trees, there were dragonflies eating clouds of mosquitoes. Several big splashes told me there were big fish swimming unseen. All in all, a pleasant place to have a quiet and relaxed paddle in a small boat.

TODAY? NOT TODAY

For this day, I took the #63 bus in Sooke for a day of commando kayaking, with my little inflatable Lagoon kayak on a roller. The #63 goes past two little lakes, Poirier and Kemp. Both are stocked with trout for fishing. This day was my first time to Kemp Lake.

It wasn't hard at all to get there from Kemp Lake Road. The bus driver let me off at the corner of Chubb Road where I could see the boat launch at the lakeshore. I walked two long blocks on pavement, past some houses and a pretty farm. There is room at the end of the road for three or four cars to park next to a large green shed which seems to be waterworks for a drinking water facility. Kemp Lake is drinking water for many local homes, so be clean and considerate paddlers here!

The boat launch itself is well-suited to kayaks and canoes, and there is a rickety little dock suitable for launching boats or swimming. A grassy space made a convenient place to inflate my kayak. Though the tiny beach has very shallow water, it's possible to launch without getting muddy. Tiny fish darted about the rocks and mud as I launched. A few minutes later, I also saw a trout about as long as my hand. Fish!

This was the day I somehow managed to take two halves of two entirely different kayak paddles. The kayak was already inflated when I made this discovery. Both paddle parts had yellow blades and black shafts, but alas, that was as similar as they got. The paddle shafts were slightly different shapes and sizes, and they wouldn't fit together. It was frustrating, but after a bus ride and a walk trundling along with my kayak, I wasn't about to let a little thing like Not Having A Paddle stop me from getting on the water.

I tried using one paddle half like a canoe paddle, and found a backwards stroke was easier to control. My little boat moved backwards nicely along the shore, and nobody came by to notice my unconventional style. I didn't have to get anywhere fast, just steer a little.

It was a day for relaxing and dawdling, so I floated in my little kayak and drifted. Turkey vultures circled overhead, bringing to mind the line from the first season of *Game of Thrones* where the dancing-master asks, "What do we say to death? Not today."

SOMETIMES I'D LIKE an origami boat.

I'd like to make my own little paper toy folded out of paper, and float it with all my thoughts and wishes going out to my late father, whose ashes were scattered at sea. Maybe I'll look through an origami website or a YouTube video and find something to make.

I'd like to make my own origami real kayak, a little rec kayak, and ride it on a calm day in a quiet place like Spectacle Lake. I had a little simple one that flattened out into an 8-foot-long shape which could fit into many kinds of passenger van. It didn't make the triage when we moved away from the Beach House. I'll make a better one instead!

I'd like to try the Oru Kayak, which seems to be an interesting form of kayak origami. It's also a useful design for commando kayaking or transporting kayaks by bike and bus and on foot. Sure wish someone would bring one to a local Paddlefest so I could try it.

For origami fans, there are other scientific discoveries about this art of folding. One recent invention is a sheet of plastic that can fold itself into two different forms. I read about it in *Scientific American* magazine! Another article in Scientific American notes that other kinds of plastic origami might be useful for shaping cells into tiny containers for future medical uses. Plastic that folds itself when an electric current runs through it? Sounds like an idea for a self-folding kayak: plug it in or turn on the battery, and bip-bend-bop the slim flat box unfolds itself and refolds itself into a kayak.

THESE DAYS, WHEN THINKING about the news of Freya Hoffmeister and her World Paddlers Award as well as Justine Curgenven's video *Kayaking the Aleutians*, I'm reminded of Jane Austen.

Yes, the novelist, who wrote *Pride and Predjudice* and *Sense and Sensibility*. No, really – there's a connection between Austen and paddling. She was interested in small boats, after all. It was in her novel *Persuasion* (released in 1816) that she wrote: "I hate to hear you talk about all women as if they were fine ladies instead of rational creatures. None of us want to be in calm waters all our lives."

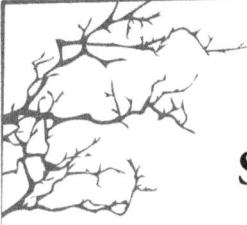

SaltSpring and Beaver

Saturday was a day for a recreational paddle on Beaver Lake. It's a sheltered lake, a small end of a roughly figure-eight shaped lake still known by two names: Elk Lake for the big loop where the rowing sculls zoom about, and Beaver Lake for the small loop where the speed of boats is generally much lower. (Yeah, yeah, they've been one lake for a hundred years since Colquitz Creek was dammed to raise the water level when this was the reservoir for Victoria. We still think of them as two lakes. Go figure.)

It was a mild winter day, so I paddled in regular clothes... well, if River Pants from MEC and an Icebreaker merino shirt qualify as "regular" then I was in civvy clothes. Actually, I wear them a lot in the winter, so there! I also took the small inflatable kayak rather than my lovely sea kayak, because I wanted to be able to take the bus home. The Necky kayak doesn't fit on the bike rack on the front of the bus, alas.

Out on the water, I noticed a flock of over a hundred coots sitting on the water. It was easy to give them lots of room, and on my way back from admiring some birds' nests and a cormorant perch at the mouth of Elk Lake, I saw the coots again. Now they were splashing with their wings, one or two birds at a time and usually at the edges of their big flotilla.

What were they up to?

After a few minutes of drifting and observing their ducking heads and splashing wings, it seemed clear that the coots were following a school of little fish and chasing the fish into the centre of their group. As the coots milled around, everybody got a chance to dip in and take a fish. I couldn't tell what kind of fish were being caught, just that they were small fingerlings.

What a day to forget my camera!

Learning Experience

SATURDAY WAS MY DAY to volunteer at the Nature House in Elk/Beaver Lake Park. The Nature House is down at the Beaver Lake end of the big, figure-eight-shaped lake that was the drinking resevoir for Victoria about a hundred years ago.

Like most days when I'm the volunteer naturalist, I took an inflatable kayakalong for the day. Usually I get to the park in the morning, set up my kayak, and get an hour or two on the water before opening the nature centre to visitors. This time was a little different.

The difference came when I lowered my Expedition, folded up in its bag and bungee-ed to a luggage roller, out of the bus. (Yup, I can take a kayak on a bus. Don't boggle. If you've been reading Kayak Yak for a while, you've seen photos of me trundling a kayak along as what looks like a big suitcase.) As I lowered it to the ground... well, maybe it fell a bit... that big puppy weighs 42 pounds, and with paddle/PFD/pump & the luggage roller it must have been over 45 pounds (call it 20+ kilos for those who think metric) and it's hard to hold it up from above. Next time I'm getting off the bus FIRST and then lowering the kayak & roller.

Ahem.

To get back to the point, a wheel broke off the luggage roller.

This was not a honking big problem. Of all the places I've taken a kayak on a roller, this was not a horrible place for the roller to break. I was able to get the kayak to the Nature House, and even take it home later in the day. And even as I did so, I was acutely aware that if the break had happened in some of the other places this kayak has been, I would have been up the proverbial creek without a proverbial paddle.

Not to gloss over the process of what it's like being up a moderately proverbial creek, I dragged my dear kayak on one wheel and a corner of the frame for the better part of a kilometre. (Note to self: the kayak that is too heavy for me to carry for more than a few steps is very nearly too heavy to drag unless it's rolling properly on two wheels.) The walk from the bus stop to the Nature House, which usually takes about eight minutes with the kayak&roller, took closer to forty minutes. I passed the time, plodding or resting, with mental additions to my List Of Rules For Kayak Carpools.

The new rules include:

-When carpooling in someone else's vehicle:

-never stink more than your driver, even after a hard day paddling

-never smoke anything that your driver didn't pass to you, lit

-always offer snacks to your driver

-always have a couple of loonies and quarters ready for parking meters, and put the coins in the change holder on the dashboard as you say, "Good! These were rattling around in my pocket."

I'm still re-phrasing what I'd like to say about the three drivers with vans and the two with pick-up trucks who passed me on that narrow lane to the parking lot by the Nature House. The drivers of tiny sedans I forgave. They all looked old and doddering, which is about what I must have looked like cresting the rise in the lane. I guess the drivers of one van and one pick-up truck will get a pass from me, because they had Handicapped symbols hanging from the rear-view mirrors and their vehicles were full.

At any rate, by the time I got to the Nature House, I had had my upper-body workout for the day, particularly because I was trying unsuccessfully to tip the frame a bit to take most of the weight on the lone wheel. This day has to be classified as my least successful commando kayaking expedition so far.

I could have been extremely grumpy, but for a spot of good luck. The lake was full of model sailboats having a tournament. Ya know, it's really really hard to be grumpy when you're looking at dozens of three-foot-high sails, particularly when they're on brightly-painted tiny yachts. I'm just sayin'.

And the last potential grumpiness evaporated when I got a phone call on my cell from Marlene, who cheerfully agreed to come meet me at the lake when my volunteer time was up. She brought her Smart Car. We have now conclusively proved that a fourtwo Smart Car can carry two adults, two small backpacks, and my Expedition kayak in its bag without crowding the driver or passenger and with PLENTY of room left over.

We plan to put TWO kayaks and gear into her Smart Car and go to SaltSpring for one day this summer.

FAILED AT FINDING A whale?

"The water is like glass this morning. You should really go out in your kayak," my partner said Monday morning, after he returned from walking our landlady's dogs. I accepted the advice, got into my wetsuit and stacked gear in my Eliza. After all, someone saw a grey whale out by Ten Mile Point on Sunday... maybe I'd be lucky and see it too!

Rolling down to the beach was fine. Gyro Park on Cadboro Bay is a great place to launch, whether you're rolling a kayak on wheels or unloading a canoe from a car roof, or hauling a rowing dinghy on a little trailer. Any changes that Saanich Parks ever makes to this park should take small boats into consideration, and make it easier rather than harder to bring a boat to the shore. (

The tide was low and still receding. Though the water wasn't quite glassy, it was a calm day. Before long I was out at Evan's Rock and looking about optimistically for a grey whale. Nope! none to be seen. Maybe it was still hanging around, but if so, it was hiding well off-shore. It would be smart not to come close to shore with the tide so low. I went along the Smuggler's Cove area over to Cadboro Point, looking at all the rocks which are normally just visible under the water.

It was a good time on the water. And even if I completely failed at seeing a whale, there were plenty of other things to see. A big eagle flew overhead. There were at least three ravens, too, and along the rocks a couple of oystercatchers were scrambling. The seal that hangs out around Flower Island seems to have a new baby this year... at least, there was a little seal head bobbing up near her head as she watched me paddle past the island. And otters! I saw three separate groups of otters out and about. Low tide is the time when the coastal buffet opens for them, and they scramble all around the rocks and through the shallow water. At one rock I saw a big white starfish among the seaweed, and a big jellyfish the colour of a poached egg.

So, no whale, but lots of other animals. That more than made up for pulling a muscle tugging my kayak up the steep ramp of soft, dry sand.

Oh, and the next morning Bernie and I walked our landlady's dogs over to Telegraph Bay and found another animal on the beach of little stones. A polychaete! In English, that's a bristly marine worm. This one looked like a big gray earthworm, like a night crawler about fourteen inches long. I found a drawing online of a polychaete. The Arenicolidae are common intertidal sandworms that look much like this one did.

The website had a page with taxonomic questions so that it was possible to figure out which particular bristly marine worm we might have found. Some of them are more bristly, others more wormy... and a few of them are freaky weird. Now, most people have less interest in marine worms than kayaks, I know. But since members of our paddle group have at different times found tube worms, fire worms, and the egg sacs of an unidentified marine worm, well, I found it interesting to look through this website. There were sketches of many families of marine worms, from the feather-duster-style tube worms to sea mice and things that are like stinging centipedes. Most of the drawings came from a book by J.H. Day, *Polychaeta of Southern Africa*, published in 1967 by the British Museum Natural History.

It would be nice to see a whale from my kayak, at a proper distance, but it's ok with me to see all these other animals that come out to play on a mild summer morning.

MEETING THE THREE WISE Men

Okay, counting the nudist it might have been four. And the strong guy, maybe five.

It's not every day I meet three wise men – or three men who think they are wise – but then, it's been about ten years since I last paddled at Salt Spring Island. On Tuesday I went commando kayaking, as Dubside calls it.

I packed up an inflatable kayak sent to me by Advanced Elements (the Expedition, their biggest solo kayak) and the Backbone sent to me by Lee Johnson, a follower of Kayak Yak and the #1 fan of Expeditions and Backbones. The gear bag has room for a take-apart four-piece paddle, a PFD, bilge pump and throwbag of rope, water bottle and a doublestroke pump the size of my thigh. (I may be short but Lord knows, I'm not tiny.)

I stuffed a little drybag with a squall jacket, merino wool Icebreaker shirt, wallet, cell phone, ball of yarn & needles and snack bars, then hopped on the bus. One transfer got me and about 48 pounds of gear all the way to the Swartz Bay ferry. I knitted a baby bootie on the way, and listened to a podcast of the CBC's radio program IDEAS, so this was a real multi-tasking kind of morning!

After trundling my gear down to Berth 3 at the terminal, I settled in to wait for the ferry to Salt Spring. A nice old coot came by, a talkative older guy who accepted a granola bar from me and then observed, "You know, I have to tell you this, miss, you really have to lose forty pounds off your waistline. And I wish you'd wear a hat." I put my hat back on and listened as he gave more advice to six people, two dogs and a bird who came by during the next half-hour.

A cloudy morning turned clear as the fog burned off and the 5km breeze blew a few sheets of cloud past all day. The weather turned out perfect – you couldn't have requisitioned better weather with a mission statement and a government grant. The crossing gave me a great view of Portland Island and Russell Island.

There was a bus stop at the Fulford Harbour ferry terminal, but no bus to Ganges was scheduled to meet this sailing. I looked around for a nearby launch spot. Both public docks had great ramps but were too high above the water. When in doubt, shop!

I stepped into The Wardrobe, a lovely little boutique full of hippie clothes, and spied one of the little velvet hats from Tibet that aren't being brought over the ocean any more. Had to have it, even if too small for me. It will fit either Erica or John just fine (Bernie's niece and nephew who paddled with us in Cadboro Bay). The store owner told me there were two beach accesses within a short walk: one to the right of the ferry (a three-metre vertical scramble down a dirt bluff) and a nice little shell beach about 500 metres down the road.

Do not believe locals anywhere who say that a beach access is less than a klick away or level access or a nice clear trail or even easy to spot from the road.

I was lucky enough to meet a dog-walking lady who agreed there was a nice little shell beach just down the road, as the store owner had told me. She and her schipperke dog walked by me into the tiny town of Fulford Harbour. I slogged up three hills (none of which my local guides had mentioned) and was half-way up another before twigging that I'd missed the trail to the beach. Half-way back, the dog-walker met me on her return. "You missed it!"

She showed me the trail. It was hidden under overgrown bushes, and made for hobbits! I bent over and crept through lovely-scented brush and trees, on a footpath barely wide enough for both my shoes, and not wide enough for the battered luggage roller with my Expedition strapped to it. Still, the brush opened up and I made it eventually to the shore along a quite pretty walk. It might be even more pleasant if one isn't walking backwards tugging a tippy 45-pound bag over uneven ground.

At the shore was a two-metre drop over steep rough rock to a perfect little shell beach. Got the gear down without either throwing it nor falling after it, and set up on shore. Bliss.

Another dog and another local arrived as I was prepping to launch, a polite older fellow. I gotta say, of all the grey-haired men of my acquaintance, he was the second-fastest at getting naked. He and the dog were in the water, swimming, before I looked up from tying my paddle leash.

This bay at Fulford Harbour confirms a trend I've noticed among several bays here at the south end of Vancouver Island and among the Gulf Islands. The bays all point in roughly the same direction – 120 degrees from magnetic north on my compass, kind of south-east. The shoreline on the north and east side of these bays is usually rocky and at a moderately steep angle to the water. The shoreline on the west and south side of these bays is usually more sloped to the water. I was on the north and east side today. It was a shoreline very like the comparable shore of Cadboro Bay, in my home waters. The biggest difference was not one but three shell beaches, only one of which is on Reserve land for the Tsawout band.

At the bend in the bay I turned round and followed the rocky shore back, appreciating the water-stained colours of the basalt and the lichens and mosses growing on the stone. Into the little harbour at Fulford, I puttered around the ferry dock and two marinas, getting well out of the way before the ferry came in. Along into the estuary and over to the far side of the bay for a few minutes, following the sound of a drum on the shore. I hopped ashore at the picnic area to check out the petroglyph held by three tree trunks. It's a fairly large carving of a face – a seal, according to the brass sign fixed nearby. Next time we come to Salt Spring I hope to make a rubbing of it.

The road runs right by the water here, and there is a roadside stand at the farm gate across the road. Hurray! Though all the eggs were sold, I had enough cash in my pocket to buy a jar of peach jelly and a little bag of handmade gift tags.

Nearby was a young man, lighting a small fire on the beach. We said hello, and then he asked me, "Do you believe in Jesus Christ, our lord and saviour?"

I said Yup. He was very happy to hear it, particularly happy for someone whose worldly goods fit into a shopping cart and whose furniture was a drum on a beach log. He was wise enough to talk about how good God was, and the world, and to say bye nicely when I paddled away across the estuary. Saw the lovely old rock church, and paddled back up to the tiny town.

Under the dock I found a tiny beach at high tide, landed and packed up my boat. I scrambled up the little bluff with some of my gear, and looked around. Some young dude was waiting for the bus or a ride, and I requested help. He very kindly put down his own pack and carried my kayak bag up to the road. One-handed, without assistance or complaints. Yay, helpful stranger!

He was kind, but the third wise man didn't make an appearance until after I'd caught the ferry back to Swartz Bay and got on the bus. A young native guy got on behind me and said, "You gotta hear this song. My friend wrote it." He sang, then chatted nicely all the way in to town while I finished knitting another bootie, and was pleased to be given the booties for his little nephew. In trade, he told me a poem, of which the only lines I can remember are:

We do not need to think our way into a better kind of living.
We need to live our way into a better kind of thinking.

Then he lifted my heavy gear bag off the bus at my stop. I got home by ten-thirty.

All in all, a good day, including the visits from three men who thought they were wise and two who were wise enough for the moment.

OPPORTUNITY

A last-minute opportunity to visit Salt Spring Island saw me putting my little inflatable kayak into Karen's van and tagging along for the ride. She was headed to Salt Spring for work, Bernie was going to visit a goat cheese dairy, and I was off to go noodling in Fulford Harbour.

This is a good place to paddle when there's little or no wind. Today there was just a slight breeze and patchy clouds as I walked off the ferry, rolling the Dragonfly on its luggage roller behind me. The tide was way out (waaaaayy out). When I looked at the little path down three metres of bluff to the beach below the public dock, there was way more beach than I needed for launching. There was not only muddy shingle, but lots of gooey mud before the water line. Maybe in an hour or two the tide would come in enough that I'd be able to land here, but launching right now would just get me muddy to the knees. For this beach, one really has to choose a moment when the tide is optimal for launching or landing.

So I went off Morningside Road to find the path to the little shell beach the locals had told me about last time I was kayaking here. Yup, it's still there of course, about a klick or two hills along the road. If you get to a big stream under the road, you've gone a little too far. There's a clump of bushes pretty much hiding a trail made for hobbits. It was way easier to pull the Dragonfly in its bag along the narrow footpath than the bigger Expedition kayak. At the shore I lowered the wheeled bag down the two-metre rocky bluff to the shell beach. The band of shell fragments was completely exposed at this low tide, and rocky shingle, but not really any mud. Score!

This beach is a really nice place, out of sight of any houses, with a great view of much of Fulford Harbour south of the ferry dock. I got the kayak inflated and stuffed my waterproof dunk bag and water bottle into it, then fastened the big pump in the rolled-up kayak bag on the back deck. On the front deck went the folded luggage roller and all the safety gear. I can tuck some of the gear inside the Dragonfly, but I've found that if someone stops to talk with me they usually don't ask things like "Don't you have any safety gear?!" if they can see my pump and throw bag on deck. It's just easier that way.

As soon as I launched, I saw a great blue heron fishing about fifty feet away. I carefully tried not to splash and scare it. The breeze had another idea though, but luckily the heron just stared at me as the waves smacked against my boat. There was a little more breeze than I liked, especially with gear strapped onto the decks of the Dragonfly. Reluctantly, I gave up the idea of following the shoreline along the First Nations land as I had done back in the fall. I just went straight around the little headland to the ferry dock.

In the harbour itself there was plenty of shelter from the wind. I noodled the little kayak around between the BC Ferry dock and the shore where I'd never have gone if the ferry were still in dock. The public dock was even more sheltered. It was nice to see the big tarred pilings holding up the dock and its ramp, and the purple seastars that were clinging to the poles. The tide was out far enough to show white and brown sea anemones at the bases of some of the poles. I tried to take photos with my cell phone but haven't got the knack that my daughter Lila has for this simple phone camera.

It was good to spend a long, slow hour or more just noodling around the marinas. The tide was too far out to let me go across the flats to Drummond Park and the petroglyph, so I just looked at the stone church on this shore instead. A boat owner chatted with me a little about how practical kayaks are because they don't need to burn fuel. "Fifty dollars an hour to take my fishing boat out!" he admitted. And he added, "See you've got your safety gear right there." Then he told me low tide was a good time to see starfish and anemones along the rocks. I wandered off to look for them, and found two more small shell beaches, one only three or four metres from side to side between the rocks. There were several little jellyfish, too – the clear moon jellies with tiny blue insides. When the ferry came in, I carefully stayed out of its way... they've got enough on their minds without hotdogging paddlers playing in their wake.

Eventually I wandered back to the shore by the public dock and was pleased to see most of the mud was now covered by water, as the tide had risen a bit. Took my time wading to shore, lifting the Dragonfly. Folded everything up, put the re-loaded bag back on its luggage roller, and then looked thoughtfully at the three-metre bluff. It's an easy climb, and I should be able to do it with the Dragonfly. But just then, the boat owner who'd been chatting with me earlier came up the steep ramp of the public dock, and offered to help with my kayak in its bag. He carried it up the bluff for me, no problem. Nice person!

And now for the post-paddling portion of the pleasant day, there was the expensive snack at a tiny coffee shop... next time, I'll just eat the granola bar in my dunk bag instead. Bernie found me sitting in the sunshine, letting my sandals dry out. Karen came back from her errands in plenty of time for the ferry. A little bit of window-shopping in the pleasant stores of Fulford Harbour, and then onto the ferry and back to Victoria.

It's always a good thing riding the ferries, even on a rainy day. This breezy day was warm and dry, and well worth taking the opportunity for just getting out and about. I know we have adventures in our kayaks some days, and someday soon we'll head out from Fulford Harbour to nearby Russell Island or Portland Island, but for today this was a good quiet time on the water.

GANGES!

No, not the holy river in India. The town on SaltSpring Island. In a masterpiece of coordinating weather and transportation, technology and nature, I was able to enjoy kayaking in Ganges Harbour. The weather report called for sunny skies in the afternoon, and a wind warning, but I left the house just after 7:00am planning to have a good day even if weather didn't let me get on the water. The clouds were enough to keep the day from getting hot, but not enough to rain. Score!

It had been been months since I was last able to visit SaltSpring, and then I was only able to putter around Fulford Harbour. Nice, but I'd done it before. This time, I was able to hop on the island's little community bus and catch a ride to Ganges. Some 14 km from Fulford, the trip to town is too far to walk while trundling the Expedition, a 35 pound kayak, bagged up with a PFD, two paddles, a big air pump and a small emergency pump, a water pump & throw bag, and a small dunk bag. I had no trouble getting the gear onto the regular transit buses in Victoria (especially when a fella helped me lift it onto the #70) or onto the ferry at Swartz Bay. But since I was the last person onto the ferry, my kayak on its luggage roller got trapped at the stern behind some tightly-parked cars. When the other foot passengers walked off and got on the community bus, I was stuck until the cars had cleared. The bus was gone by then, but no problem. It was nice to poke around in Fulford for a while.

Waiting for the bus gave me time to go into Rock Salt (a lovely little bistro) and eat some of their excellent chocolate mousse. This isn't the only cafe or restaurant in the village, but it's the one I like best. And they'll fill your water bottle without charging you an arm & a leg! And around the corner, past the post office, is the best place to find sundresses and scarves.

After shopping a little and walking around, I read a local magazine till the bus came. The kayak case was almost too big to wrestle onto the bus, but with a little help I got it onto the front seat where it rode in splendour, stared at by all the bus passengers. The bus driver Don was very helpful, and even suggested that I use the boat ramp next to Centennial Park in Ganges' small "downtown" area. The ramp was perfect for my purposes. I hustled onto the water, not wanting to linger on the ramp. Wet tracks showed that this ramp was in use already that morning.

Just outside the breakwater is Grace Island, with a shell beach that's exposed at low tide. So neat to look at the tons of crumbling shell and realize that people have been eating clams and oysters here since before the Pyramids were built in Egypt!

There's a lot of traffic in Ganges Harbour... cormorants, seals, and ravens as well as the kind of traffic that treats kayaks like speedbumps. I'm used to sailboats and motorboats of various kinds, but the Harbour Air floatplane certainly had the right-of-way as far as I was concerned. I got out of the heavy traffic channel quickly, and popped over to Goat Island.

Here my cell phone came in good use. Nice to be able to let Bernie know that I did get to SaltSpring like I'd hoped, and that I planned to be on the 3:40 ferry back from Fulford Harbour. Plus, I took a photo of the lacey sandstone rock, weathered by the waves. All through this conversation and drifting, a great blue heron kept on fishing from a rock on the other edge of a tiny cove. Go heron!

My SPOT device sent out an OK message, when I pushed the button at the other end of Goat Island, the south end, at exactly 48.8483 latitude, -123.47523 longitude. The message is supposed to be reassuring to friends & family that I am OK on the water. But it also seems to serve as a bit of crowing with delight, "I'm on the water! And letting you know about it, even if you're at work or home with a cold!"

I looked across a channel at Deadman Island, knowing there was just time to nip across and back before beginning a leisurely return along Goat Island back towards the shore. But then, a seal popped up and stared at me. I paused to send the OK message on my SPOT. The seal popped up again and stared even harder. Y'know, this was really the seal's place. I didn't have to go past it to see that other island for a moment. I'll go see it some other time. Better to head back early when I'm paddling alone. It was nice to take my time looking at the wave-worn shore and the arbutus trees, and another float plane roaring past.

My cell phone rang at Grace Island, on my way back to shore. Bernie checked in, and made sure that I knew about the wind warning. The gusts had just hit at Victoria, and he knew it wouldn't be long till the weather front made it north to Ganges Harbour. I reassured him that I was ten minutes from the boat ramp. Technology is our friend at moments like this! And for sure, half an hour later while I was onshore packing up the Expedition in a leisurely way, the wind started to pick up.

With everything packed, I trundled the roller along to the Visitors Info Centre where the buses all stop. Got out my knitting and did a few more rows on the latest project. Wrestled onto the bus, rolled onto the ferry, and enjoyed a day that had turned sunny & bright when the wind came howling in. Cruise ships don't come any better than this, lounging on the upper deck with people getting windburned brown and seals below surfing in the waves. What a day!

ON THE FERRY

Making up for not being out in my kayak this morning is the fact that we're on the water anyway – on a vessel rated to carry tons instead of the 1 or 2 passengers of our kayaks. Bernie and I are on the ferry from Swartz Bay to Tsawassen, going to meet his dad on the mainland for the day. Walked on, carrying a little bag each, and now we're set up with a newspaper, computer, cookies from home and our hot drink mugs.

It's just a day trip, not a grand adventure. But as I sit at a carrel and swivel to look out the port side windows and the starboard windows, I can see Russell Island between me and Fulford Harbour on SaltSpring Island on one side, and Portland Island on the other side. These two little islands are gems in the chain that is the Gulf Islands National Park Reserve.

Some people save up all year to take this trip. Some people read magazines and dream about paddling here. Bernie and I are lucky enough to be here, on a grey day with the clouds socking in around Mount Tuam and the sea the colour of steel. There are seals on the rocks at the shore of Portland, and a dozen beaches along the SaltSpring shore ...

There's Ganges Harbour, where we have to paddle again. Soon we'll pass Prevost Island, and go into Active Pass. I'm so full of plans for paddling this summer. Day trips, eh? and maybe an overnight on Galiano at Montague Harbour. Meanwhile, this gray day is a great day even though the water is too far away to touch.

(later)

Excellent meeting on the mainland – everybody was happy enough that this carbon-expensive day was more than worth it.

On the way back through Active Pass, Bernie saw a large seal and I saw four sea kayaks close to Miners Bay on the Mayne Island side. Hope it was a safe paddle for them!

PLANNING FOR APPLEFEST

We had such a good time at Applefest before. I wish I had time to go again this fall. But this year, V-Con science fiction conference is happening that same weekend, and my daughter is bringing her newlywed husband to visit Victoria. So, no Applefest for me. Instead, we'll take the new son-in-law out in Cadboro Bay in the kayaks.

Applefest is a great reason to visit SaltSpring Island, so maybe next year. Another good reason is paddling in Fulford Harbour or Ganges Harbour. But for that, we'll have to see who is interested either in driving onto the ferry with kayaks on their vehicle roofs, or walking on and trundling one of my inflatable kayaks behind them.

Next year, I wonder if the weather will be good enough to camp the night at the campground in Ganges... October is sometimes pretty cold, especially if it rains.

If you haven't been to an Applefest, check out their videos on YouTube.

THINK ABOUT GRACE ISLET as a paddler

Grace Islet is a small rocky island with scrubby short trees, found in Ganges Harbour. It's a funeral island, a traditional graveyard for the Coast Salish people. I wish I could show you the photo I took from the water while paddling there, but it's on my old phone and inaccessible ... At least I can share what I wrote on the blog about this lovely little island three years ago:

Just outside the breakwater is Grace Island, with a shell beach that's exposed at low tide. So neat to look at the tons of crumbling shell and realize that people have been eating clams and oysters here since before the Pyramids were built in Egypt!

John and Louise have paddled past this little island, on their kayaking vacation in April 2012. Alison saw it from the shore of Ganges Harbour on her kayaking vacation that year, but didn't get to paddle around it like the rest of us.

Now the owner of the island hatched a plan to build a house there, right among the First Nations traditional burial cairns and open sites. While he intended to build it on stilts over the remains, any house would cover most of this little islet. These house-building plans have inspired the formation of the **Grace Islet Community** to call for protected status for this island as a historical First Nations gravesite. Their members were speaking at a board meeting of the Capital Regional District. Personally, I wrote to the CRD already on this issue because I am a volunteer naturalist for the CRD, saying briefly:

I have paddled around Grace Islet with my kayak. I respect this traditional place and urge you to preserve it as a historical site, a graveyard, a bird sanctuary, or whatever legislation will keep it unspoiled by the misuse of the current construction project.

thank you,

Paula Johanson

CRD volunteer

Update – Good News! Grace Islet Community updated their website page with news that the CRD board has unanimously passed a motion saying:

> HEREFORE BE IT RESOLVED THAT the Capital Regional District Board requests that the Ministry of Forest Lands and Natural Resources Operations Archaeology Branch suspend the Alteration Permit issued for Grace Islet, Saltspring Island Electoral Area, to allow consultation and negotiations to proceed between First Nations, the Provincial government and the landowner to ensure protection of this First Nations cultural heritage site. AND BE IT FURTHER RESOLVED THAT the Capital Regional District Board direct staff to convene an inter-governmental meeting in the autumn of 2014 with representatives of First Nations, the Archaeology Branch, the Islands Trust and the CRD to restore trust and identify specific improvements to development approval procedures that will increase protection of First Nations cultural heritage sites within the Capital Region.

And you can write to your local Member of the Legislative Assembly or Member of Parliament if you have an opinion of your own. Since we paddlers are some of the people who pass by this little island and enjoy it without damaging it, we can be good neighbours who can speak to our government representatives about how to manage it as a responsible community.

MIRAGES

It's always nice to get out on the water during a cold winter day. For one thing, if it's sunny and bright the day doesn't feel clammy and chill. For another, odds are it's been cold and rainy for the last while, so getting out is a nice change. And the bottom line is, paddling is a nice change from trying to bake Christmas cookies that just haven't been working out right this year.

The other day, sometime before Christmas, I looked out the window and saw there was little or no breeze disturbing the big willow tree in the front yard. Moments later, I was in my wetsuit and paddle jacket, pumping up my Dragonfly inflatable kayak.

Once down on Cadboro Bay beach, I looked out at the Chain Islets... or tried to. The horizon looked a little funny. Though the tide was not all the way in, the little islets were invisible, something that shouldn't happen when I'm standing on the shore. Great Chain didn't appear as big as it usually does. I squinted at the horizon, launched my kayak, and squinted at the horizon again from this new angle, eyes only about two feet above the water. It must have been a mirage! Usually when a mirage happens around here, on a bright day, the effect makes little rocks and islands on the horizon look taller, not shorter. Sometimes the horizon stretches to absurd amounts, or there are upside-down images of sailboats merrily sailing along on top of the real ones. But not this day; objects along the horizon were compressed and obscured instead.

I paddled along the shore past the little rock garden, Sheep Cove and Stein Island and out to Flower. Through the channel I could feel a breeze that had been blocked by the long bulk of the point, and I could see the light at Cadboro Point. The freight train was running, as the tide was coming in.

Hoo doggies, was the freight train running! There were standing waves visible here, four or five hundred metres away. I could see the waves curling and frothing, and it looked like they were about half a meter high. But wait a minute... that couldn't be right. Standing waves wouldn't normally be that high unless there was a much stronger wind than this breeze, blowing against the current.

It took a minute to remember the odd mirage I'd seen at the shoreline. This was another mirage! But now, it was acting more like the usual mirage, stretching an image at the horizon so the standing waves looked much higher than they actually were.

Probably. I wasn't about to paddle over there and have a good look from close up, not in my 8 1/2 foot inflatable when I was out on my own, no matter how good the weather. That was enough of an outing for one day, so I went back to shore. Made another batch of cookies that just didn't work right – dry and hard – but heck, it was still the holiday season, even so. Peace on Earth, goodwill to all.

THERE'S PADDLING INFORMATION everywhere!

I've been reading a book called *Transporters: Contemporary Salish Art*. It's published by the Art Gallery of Greater Victoria. This is a terrific read, with strong and beautiful images. If you're living in Victoria, you can go read the copy at the Greater Victoria Public Library. If you live somewhere else, go ask your local public library to get a copy. Hey, get yourself a copy at your local bookstore!

It's hard to imagine a book on Salish Art that wouldn't mention boats and paddling on the local waters. And this book has some brilliant moments. Among these moments are names for four different kinds of canoes, in the version of the Salish language spoken on the Saanich Peninsula, SENĆOŦEN (pronounced Sen-chah-then).

There are two words defined in the text of the book *Transporters* that are very appropriate for paddlers to know. I'll quote them directly from the book, using the glossary written by STOLC/EL-, John Elliot. The first word is:

S,IST

This word has a very big meaning and refers to wherever you go in your canoe to hunt, fish, and sustain your life. This is where beliefs, knowledge, and environmental laws are passed on. This is related to cultural survival and maintaining relationships to ancestral lands and sacred responsibilities.

Now *that's* a word I needed.

And the second word is:

SJELC/A.SEN_

The moon of December. This is the time to thank your paddle and put it away. Talking to it like a reliable friend, thank your paddle for taking you where you needed to go for your life. Tell it that you will return soon to pick it back up for travelling back to sea, to your S,IST

In winter, both of these words are in my thoughts and on my mind.

Red Deer

Rally at Songhees
    Well, the weather blew, it shone and it snowed. And that was before Bernie and I went on the water.

We turned up one afternoon at Ocean River's dock on the Upper Harbour for the rally against a proposed marina for mega-yachts in the Inner Harbour. Yes, Victoria's harbour has a confusing series of names, starting with the Outer Harbour, the Inner Harbour, the Upper Harbour and on through the Selkirk Water and the Gorge to Portage Inlet (which is an odd thing to call a tidal salt-water lake). But I digress.

When Ocean River put out the call to their e-mailing list about the rally, the note included a promise that rental kayaks would be available at no charge for those attending the rally. This was a terrific offer – I'd recommend that anyone planning to rent a kayak consider renting from Ocean River as a "thank you!" for these free rentals. I booked a double right away, figuring Bernie and Lila would use it and I'd follow along in an inflatable.

But as Bernie and I hopped off the bus and trudged along with two knapsacks full of paddle gear for us and Lila (and the Dragonfly trundling along as well) we felt a distinct chill and a stiff breeze. "Let's go down this way, close to the bridge," Bernie said, "and get a look at the water before we get to Ocean River." We could see whitecaps off our launch beach at Songhees.

Lila doesn't paddle often, and was allowed to back out of paddling this windy day. She became our ground crew instead, guarding the packs and inflatable at a Chinatown restaurant. "No, Mom, you can't take your little boat out there," she insisted. "It will be a balloon." It's so nice when kids grow up and start looking after you...

The Upper Harbour was pretty well sheltered, behind Songhees Point, but it was still choppy. Bernie said the wind was gusting to 40 klicks. We geared up and launched the big Libra XT double, which we'd never tried before. That made today a boat demo as well. It's always interesting to try a new model, and this one had never been rented before.

I don't know if we'll try it again, either. Maybe on a calm day. But it sure wasn't the boat for us on this windy day – it felt like we were trying to paddle one of the container ships we see going through the Strait of Juan de Fuca. The Libra XT has a big deck humped high between the paddlers. It felt like it caught every gust of wind.

We couldn't turn that barge for love nor money till the wind faltered for a moment. The Libra came around slowly and reluctantly. It was all we could do to keep from being blown onto the rocky shoreline. When the Libra returned to its dock below Ocean River, we took that as a sign and got out.

So, out of the two dozen or so kayaks we saw gathering for the rally, our part was an abbreviated one, taking in about two hundred yards of conditions we would have enjoyed in our own boats but just couldn't take in this one. I feel like such a jam tart, when others were sporting in the waves and all; but I did hear one paddler in a surf ski comment to her friend about how careful she was being in these conditions.

We weren't the only paddlers who had a brief participation in the water part of the rally. One of the people launching managed to flip his rental kayak about ten feet off the dock and wet exited. His dignity was harmed more than anything else. Of course it was the only guy wearing blue jeans instead of paddling clothes! But he scrambled onto the dock and was helped into the boatshed immediately, out of the wind.

What a day for a rally scheduled to be on the water! And what better way to celebrate International Women's Day as well, than at a rally speaking out for the environmentally-sustainable use of our Inner Harbour?

LILA WRITES: PAULA Paddles the Red Deer River

My mother, Paula Johanson, has long dreamed of kayaking the Red Deer River and seeing in person some of the amazing places where so many fossils have been found over the years. Well, we helped launch her on Sunday and from the mud flats and intense heat we encountered it is no surprise why this area is fossil central!

I will let her be the one to post most of the details of her route and why she chose to paddle as she did, but here are the basics. She is in her mid-size inflatable kayak, (I don't know the length but it's somewhere around 13ft). She launched about 25km east of Red Deer and is expecting to land in Drumheller four days after starting. Her paddle plan has her doing 6hrs on the water each day, but she has been making excellent time so far and was already more than halfway after only 24hrs.

So far she reports the trip has been excellent. She managed to setup camp about 5min before a small thunderstorm and didn't even get soaked! She has said there are tonnes of people on the river, which is good for her safety (kayaking alone, even with a SPOT transponder is so dangerous!) but takes away some of the tranquil alone time she was hoping for.

Setting up on a busy campground beach was pretty funny. We answered dozens of questions of curious locals while their wet dogs shook water all over her gear. But the instant she hit the water, she forgot all about us and just exploded away.

Looking at the river as we setup to launch, I can certainly see the appeal. It was beyond beautiful out there, and I hope she is having the paddle of her life! I go to meet her in Drumheller on Wednesday, and will try to bring my laptop with us to Calgary so I can post pictures of her triumphant return as well.

If you look carefully at the photo on Kayak Yak website, there is a teeny, tiny dot left of center at the curve in the river. That is Paula only a few moments after launching. She was more than ready to leave us, and the blisteringly hot beach, far behind!

RED DEER RIVER

What a joy it is, to plan a paddling trip, and finally be able to do it! For a couple of years now, I've been hoping to paddle on the Red Deer River between the cities of Red Deer and Drumheller. For one thing, this stretch of river is apparently the most congenial for novice kayakers – and when it comes to white-water kayaking, I'm a novice. The video that Bernie posted of me paddling a little rough water on the Sooke River shows the only place I've put a kayak in a bumpy river.

For another thing, I am fascinated by the study of dinosaurs. And the Red Deer River is a natural highway for the study of dinosaur fossils! The Royal Tyrrell Museum in Drumheller is one of the world's finest.

Best of all, the Advanced Elements kayak that I used was ideally suited to the river, the travelling, and the paddler. I used their Expedition model, a 13-foot inflatable kayak that can travel on airplanes without being classed as over-size or over-weight baggage. (Hint: Though the bag will allow one to stuff a doublestroke air pump, a bilge pump, a throw bag, and a four-piece paddle in with the kayak, the bag will then weigh well over 50 lbs. Unless you get a nice friendly attendant at the counter, the airline will add an over-weight baggage charge.) This is a kayak I commonly take on city buses, by strapping the bag to a luggage roller like it is in the photo below.

For the last few years, I've been reading all kinds of resources on paddling the Red Deer river by canoe or kayak. There's a very helpful resource online at Paddle Alberta website, with information on several rivers. Their page on the Badlands section of the Red Deer river is terrific! I printed it out and used it as my primary information source. I also picked up a copy of the Middle Red Deer River Map at Mountain Equipment Co-op. There are also several promotional websites from park programs or chamber of commerce sites and the like.

All that preparation meant that I had a good idea what to expect on this stretch of the river, between Content Bridge and Drumheller. I borrowed a small tent from my daughter Lila, and brought my summer-weight sleeping bag. A tiny air mattress made the ground very comfortable! The yellow ten litre size drybag held my food... about three times what I needed. Hot weather = loss of appetite.

Lila and her friend Sapphira were my ground crew for this trip. Sapphira drove us from Edmonton to Red Deer to visit with the BatBaby (ask Lila about her goddaughter!) and fill my water bottles. Following the river for several miles, we arrived at Content Bridge campground. This is a good point to start a quiet paddle on the river, as there are several riffles and very easy rapids just downstream from the city of Red Deer. I didn't want the challenge or the longer trip this summer. All reports say that below this bridge, there's only the one riffle at Backbone. The $5 parking and launching fee at the campground wasn't out of line. After watching me launch, Sapphira and Lila were able to get something to eat at the burger stand.

At the shore, there were waders and dogwalkers galore who stopped to take a look at the kayak. It only takes about ten minutes to set it up and inflate it. Today I stuffed in the various drybags and pulled them out to try them in different arrangements, at least three times. This time was spent, as usual, answering questions about the boat and my gear. The technical aspects of the inflatable kayak fascinate some people. Others are concerned whether I am wearing a life jacket and carrying all the right safety gear. Even those who don't know what a throw bag is are reassured to see that there is one on my boat's deck! The SPOT device clipped to my PFD made a big impression, as I pushed the button to send an OK message with my location to my friends.

Sapphira proved a conscientious ground crew at this point. "Where's your bailer?" she asked, and I showed her the bilge pump. Several questions later, she was satisfied with my preparations. A quick goodbye to my ground crew and I climbed into my kayak with feet that were wet but not muddy.

I headed off into the hot afternoon, immediately feeling much cooler on the water than on the shore. Hurray!

I think that feeling of "hurray!" was sustained for the next four days.

The shoreline was much greener than is common in Alberta for August, but that was because of all the rain this summer. This part of the river passes through Aspen Parkland. Most of the trees and brush growing along the banks were willows... low and scrubby or twenty feet tall and bushy. Along parts of the bluffs there was sagebrush growing. After a few turns of the river that was headed southward, there were gusts of good smell on the breeze. Around another bend was a big stand of pine trees, putting out that good scent. So fresh! There was one deer standing along the shore that first afternoon, and a second deer the next day. I think they were both mule deer, as they were rather large, with dark ears.

The tension went out of me as I realized that the gentle current really was easy to handle. I practised crossing the river, doing ferries and sideslips, getting used to handling the loaded kayak in the slight current. The only time I nearly tipped was when I leaned back to watch an osprey soaring. Suddenly, it dove down and grabbed for a fish. If the osprey caught anything, the fish was too small to see with my bifocals tucked away in a drybag.

That first afternoon, I was worried about being too slow on the river. I didn't stop for dinner till I camped, and I didn't stop to camp until after making my way through the only riffle on this part of the river. It didn't sound like a "riffle" when I was approaching it. To be honest, it sounded very noisy indeed. The map and river guide both said to take the left channel around an island. The river was very shallow here at Backbone Riffle, where Anthony Henday and a party of First Nations guides crossed the river in 1745.

Most of the channel was knee-deep or less. The water ran noisily over rounded rocks. At one point, the boat bottomed out and got hung up on a rock... but the rock seemed pretty round. I was able to hop the boat along and off the rock in a few tense moments. The rock didn't leave any visible scratches on the bottom of the hull.

That was the only place where the current felt strong. Everywhere else, the current kept up a steady gentle push. In a few places it was very easy to paddle a short way upstream. If I didn't paddle, the boat would gently drift sideways and I could look back upriver to see what the weather might be doing.

The prevailing winds in central Alberta come out of the north-west. A cloud bank slowly moved in over a couple of hours, showing me that a weather front was approaching. When I heard a rumble of thunder, I turned again to see sheet lightning flashing from cloud to cloud, and rain slanting out of a cloud to the north. There would be rain here soon, within half an hour! It was time to camp.

Luckily, at that bend in the river was a perfect spot to camp: a shore easy to land, a raised bank with willow trees where I could put the tent, and a high bluff above and across the river to take most of the lightning. There was a cabin among the trees, with a firepit that smelled of recent burning, but no one was around when I called out my hellos.

There was a lot to get done in the next few minutes. I hauled the kayak up on shore and pulled out the bag with the tent. Up it went in a few minutes – not bad for the first time I'd put up this particular tent! Inside went my drybags with food, sleeping bag, and clothes. I lifted one end of the kayak, then the other, onto the bank in case the river level rose suddenly, and rolled the kayak over to keep out the rain. The nearest tree to tie it to was sixty feet away. based on tying a 15-foot painter to a 50-foot rope from my throw bag. It looked like the kayak was a dog tugging at the end of a very long leash!

Just as I got into the tent, the rain started pattering down. It was only a short squall, but I was inside and dry and snug. There was hot water in my thermos, so I made instant mashed potatoes and drank cocoa, and felt good. Lightning and thunder were no problem here. By the time it was dark, everything was quiet.

Next morning, I didn't rush to take down camp. The map seemed pretty clear, and I thought the Trenville Campground would be about an hour downstream. It was a good idea not to rush. The day was bright and clear, and when the sun finally rose over the bluffs the air quickly got hot. By then I had my gear packed up and the boat back at the shore, without rushing or trying to lift everything at once. Some people use up all their enthusiasm in a lot of heavy lifting and rushing around.

When Trenville Park campground came into view, I landed. I had to guess; they don't have a sign at the shore announcing the campground. This photo is from the Content Bridge, but it gives a sense of the green shore and the people cheerfully coming down to the water's edge... though the bridge at McKenzie Crossing is out of sight almost an hour downstream from Trenville Park!

I was really impressed by the campground at Trenville Park. The restrooms were well-maintained, and it looks like a lot of RV and truck campers like to stay here. The pay phone worked, and I was able to check in with Bernie. Two important points got confirmed: I had successfully navigated the only rough water on this part of the river, and my wallet was left in Sapphira's car. No fear though – I had a doubloon tucked into my bra, so I wasn't broke.

Cheerfully, I headed off for what promised to be a day of exciting topographical changes. The river passed under McKenzie Crossing Bridge and into Dry Island Buffalo Jump Park. It was amazing to watch the transition from Aspen Parkland to Badlands, and to see the layers in the soft bluffs that began to tower overhead. Millions of years ago, all this area was the bottom of a shallow inland sea that geologists call the Bearpaw Sea. The great black line I could see across the hills was marking out the boundary between the Cretaceous Period and the Triassic. Below that line are dinosaur bones. Above it, there are no more fossils of dinosaurs.

Any vegetation was sprinkled over the rough ground like an afterthought. Groves of pine trees continued, but were broken up by more bare ground as Badlands began to predominate. I began to smell and see herds of cattle grazing along the river banks. There were black and red Angus cows with their blocky, square calves, as well as Herefords and Charolais. Marvelous to see their various colours and hear their quiet calls to each other! Through the scrubby willows along the shore, the cattle would push through to come down to the water and drink.

The map of my second day's travels shows that I went through Dry Island Buffalo Jump Park and camped near Tolman Bridge. The spot marked 4 on the next map shows where I looked at the buffalo jump and the mesa called Dry Island. It's impressive if you know what you're looking at; a cliff becomes a cliff where the buffalo would fall, not just a crumbly bluff. And below wasn't just a jumble of muddy crumbles mixed with old bones. It was the place where people would have been waiting with spears to finish off the buffalo, after the runners had driven them off the cliff. Falling a hundred feet onto its head doesn't kill a buffalo. But the fall does stun it or break a leg, so it's easier to kill. And then, there's lots of water here from the river and a nearby stream, for the butchering and cooking. Eroded hillsides looked like dinosaur bones sticking out of the clay and sand. Some eroded bluffs along the river banks have round faces like Mount Rushmore, and others have sharp broken edges like profiles of faces looking up-river at the Buffalo Jump.

The point on the map marked 5 is where I stopped at a stream with a sandbar, to cook my dinner. I realized that for two days I'd eaten very little. Big bowl of pasta with tomato paste and parmesan... yum! Two big red Angus cows came along the shore to investigate what i was doing. You can also see this map on a satellite image just below, showing the transition from green hills above the river valley to badlands. Point 6 is where I decided to camp for the night, stopping about 7 pm instead of 8 pm like the day before. No need to rush. I passed four groups of young people or families on the river that day, drifting along on inner tubes or inflatable dinghies.

When I set up camp, I figured that the Tolman Bridge was about an hour away, but it was only ten minutes downstream. This shore was a good place to camp, though: shallow place to beach the kayak, bank to camp near trees, and a high ridge across the river in case there was lightning like last night. The weather was turning cloudy and threatening rain. There was still traffic on the river, though. Two more inner tube parties drifted by, looking to be picked up at the Bridge, and two girls on horses rode past my camp. Luckily, nobody came by when I went wading in the river and scattered tiny fishes with my splashing.

I sat in the tent, mosquitoes safely OUTSIDE, and opened my thermos for hot water to make some mashed potatoes and later some hot cocoa. Nice to have the sound of birds in the trees, and to have trees overhead in case a storm came by. That night, thunder woke me seven times before I lost count of the crack and BOOM overhead.

The map of my third day's travels shows that from Tolman Bridge I went through the Badlands, reached Starland Campsite and camped downstream from the Morrin Bridge. I woke early to the sound of wind. No need to get up right away, so I lay around letting the day's weather get better. Realized that I was still underfed, so I boiled water and made a big bowl of oatmeal with raisins and brown sugar. The sun finally came over the ridge and the day baked bright and calm. A big white pelican flew downstream. Ducks on the river today, all day, quiet and fishing and flying.

That morning, I had to wash gumbo mud off my feet and sandals when launching. No way I wanted to paddle around with a pound of mud clinging to each foot! The kayak was still rather grubby inside, but at least it wasn't slimed with clay. Some of Lila's photos on Kayak Yak show me trying to fit the luggage roller in, before unzipping the back of the kayak and putting the roller under my big drybag. Heavy things go on the bottom whenever possible!

Just below the Tolman Bridge, I found a path to the campsite. Their watertap was a "boil to drink" tap, but a nice couple in a camper gave me a litre and a half of drinking water. And here, I saw two rabbits! Little cottontails that ran when they saw me.

In places along this stretch, the river feels like it's in a canyon. This is the most isolated part of the river... there are cattle grazing on ranchlands, but no cabins visible from the river.

I planned to stop at Starland Campgrounds for water. This was a cool day, but on a hot day it's easy to need twice as much water as expected. Lila loaned me a waterbag, and Ben gave me a new metal water bottle, so I had plenty of containers.

The tea-coloured river kept moving along, and I often drifted rather than paddling. The river guide suggests to make this a short day. There was no rush. I kept an eye out for the island that would mark where to look for Starland

Campground. Even though I stopped at their boat launch, I thought it was a rancher's water access and continued on. A kilometre down the river, I could see Morrin Bridge! Suddenly, I realized that I'd passed the only available drinking water place for miles. I was lucky to find that the current was very mild here, and I was able to paddle upstream for a kilometre back to the boat launch. Up a steep path, I found the campground. It was a nice, clean place, but hot and very open with fewer trees than would be comfortable for shelter. The grass was being mowed by a woman on a tractor, who didn't mind at all me filling a couple of my water bottles.

It was too early to camp, and I didn't have the fees for camping at Starland. I went on under the Morrin Bridge to look for two possible sites on the map. I wanted a place that had a good landing, room among willows and near trees for the tent, and a big ridge either above or right across the river in case there would be more thunderstorms. (There were no storms that night, but a very heavy dew and fog in the morning.)

The first place I picked on the map had already been occupied by a group camping along the river. There were two adults and 6 boys and girls, all happy to be here. They weren't noisy, though, so I set up around the point, using a cattle trail to get up the bank for a place to put my tent. It was a good spot. The local beaver thought so, too! Several times that evening and the next morning, there was a loud slap! on the water as the beaver expressed some of his opinions about me camping there or maybe it was the group around the point. I had some opinions, too, about me camping there. Beavers are generally pretty shy when humans approach, but sleeping in a tent near those fifty-pound rats did make me think.

Morning was cool, and grey when I woke early. Fog filled the narrow valley of the river! I went back to bed with a Dick Francis novel and fell back asleep. The campers got on the river a little before I did, but I caught up to them a little above the Bleriot Ferry. There's a great sign on the river so that paddlers will know the ferry is ahead. I passed the Bleriot Ferry, and arrived in Drumheller that afternoon. Meanwhile, Lila kept checking my SPOT messages, and realized that I'd get to Drumheller before she and Sapphira were due there!

What a good day this was! I took time to drift and float often. There was another mesa along this part of the river. I love how sounds echo off the mesas and bluffs.

A couple launched their red canoe, and for about two hours paddled a few hundred yards ahead of me. The last half hour, we paddled together and talked. This was their first trip in their new canoe! Their old canoe had been stolen a few years ago, when they left it on the beach in Drumheller overnight. A little riffle came up on the last bit of the river, and they insisted that I had to run it with them, as it was the most fun part of the day. They were right – it was just bouncy enough to be fun! And then we pulled onto the beach in Newcastle Park in Drumheller.

(NOTE: Land here! There is no other place good for landing in Drumheller, as far as I can tell.)

The nice couple asked what I was doing with my gear now. I sent a text to Lila, and got a note back saying that she'd be in Drumheller that evening. Hearing that, the nice couple said that they'd give me a ride to the campground... could I watch their canoe while they went to pick up the vehicle they left at their launch point? Of course! And not only did the wife give me and my packed-up gear a ride to River Grove Campground, she waited to be sure I had a cabin rented. Awesome!

The cabin worked better than taking three separate campsites in different parts of the campground. I set up the tent on the deck, where it began evaporating dry from the morning's fog. Hand-washed all my camping clothes and hung them to dry on the picnic table. Put water to chill in the little fridge. Took out the doubloon and bought four big Freezies in the campground office. By the time that Lila and Sapphira arrived, the gear was all dry, and I'd found a little home-cookin' restaurant called The Old Grouch just two short blocks away that had plenty of vegetarian food for Sapphira and wheat-free food for Lila. We took takeout and went back to the cabin, talked till late, and slept like logs. Well, I did. When Sapphira left the tent where she'd been sleeping on a stack of air mattresses to come through the cabin in search of the bathroom, I didn't hear a thing.

I'm glad to say that by the end of this trip I hadn't pulled any muscles or strained anything. Except maybe the balls of my feet. I'd been pressing my sandals pretty hard against the footbar of the kayak for four days. Kept wanting to feel connected to the boat, and be aware of how it was moving in the current.

A terrific river trip! Glad to make the run at last.

BIRD SIGHTINGS ON THE Red Deer River

This August I had an excellent opportunity to do birdwatching while kayaking in a new place! Here's a google map I made using the SPOT messages I sent while on the Red Deer River.

The first day of four I spent on the river, though the direction of flow was generally heading south from Content Bridge there were several bends in its direction. If I stopped paddling, the current would gradually turn the kayak sideways. I turned round during the late afternoon to look back upstream at the approaching weather front. Over the river, an osprey was soaring and turning. I'm pretty darned sure it was an osprey (*Pandion balietus*) because its white underside and dark wings were visible against the sky. And as I was watching, it stooped suddenly and plunged down to the river. If it caught a fish, then the fish was too small for me to see without my glasses as the osprey flew away. This was the only time I nearly fell out of my kayak, as I was leaning back to watch the osprey and was abruptly reminded about balance and so on just before tipping.

A little later, I heard thunder rumbling and turned round again to look at the weather approaching from the north-west. It was thunder, and lightning flashed in the clouds. There was rain falling from a cloud that should take about half an hour to reach me. It was time to find a place to set up camp for the night! Luckily, there was a nice level place above the river shore just at that bend of the river. I pulled up onto the shore, walked across the level ground to another rise, calling out to the cabin that stood there. The fire pit smelled like a fire had been burning yesterday. But no one came out of the cabin. With no one around for me to ask permission, I resolved to camp here above the high water mark and try to leave no trace.

Quickly, I set up Lila's tent close to the trees and put my gear inside. Then I moved the kayak higher on the bank and rolled it upside-down. The nearest tree to tie the kayak to was sixty feet away, by the tent. It took using both the throw bag rope and my stern line, but I got that boat tied down! Strong gusts of wind are common and can easily roll a boat around. There were no gusts of wind that night, just lightning, thunder, and rain for the early evening.

On the evening of the second day, I saw a pelican. An American white pelican, or *Pelicanus erythrorhynchos*, according to the Sibley Field Guide to Birds of Western North America. Astonishing! A bird that's as long from beak to tail as I am tall – well, an inch shorter, but wow! It's as long as the Mute Swans that we see swimming and nesting in Portage Inlet. At 108 inches of wingspan, a white pelican has wings that are getting close to twice as wide as its length. It flies more quietly than a duck, with great swoops of its wings like a heron. The next morning, it flew past my camp again on its way downriver past Tolman Bridge.

The third day, there were ducks galore between Tolman Bridge and Morrin Bridge. Several small ducks looked like cinnamon teal ducks, little round bobbing things that get deftly out of the way when a paddler comes near. They weren't crowded or in flocks like at Cadboro Bay... these seemed to be living here for the summer and spread out thinly here in the Badlands.

This was the stretch of the river most isolated from humans, and there were few trees except the scrubby willows where the banks were lower. Some of the bluffs were almost like cliffs, and there were holes like those where cliff swallows or purple martins like to nest. Some holes were bigger, and set apart or entirely alone. Could a few of these holes held Wood duck nests? I'm guessing that some of these bigger holes held owls or maybe bats, though I saw neither. By the time the evenings were dark enough for owls or bats to come out, I was tucked away inside the tent and only came out to feed the mosquitoes. Any reports that mosquitoes are endangered species are not to be believed. This summer I was a participant in a Blood Donor Drive for mosquitoes and gave at least two units of whole blood... one tiny bite at a time.

On the fourth day there were no birds visible in the foggy morning. A beaver slapped the water, but I couldn't see him or any birds. Back to bed with a Dick Francis novel and a granola bar. When the fog lifted I got packed up and on the water. I couldn't identify the few birds visible from the river that day, as they were small dark blurs that didn't hang around. There were more nesting holes in the bluffs, though, so I'm guessing these were swallows. Was sad not to see any magpies, as they're pretty and smart birds common in farmland in Central Alberta. Maybe next time.

ELVIS

Our son Ben was in town this fall for a couple of weeks. It's a bit like having Elvis on tour, if Elvis ever walked 5km just to loosen up or climbs Mount Tolmie to unwind in the evenings. And if Elvis had a beard or went kayaking. This is the third (or more?) time that Ben has made his way out from Edmonton via unconventional means, from bicycling to hitch-hiking to walking.

Yep, walking. This summer, Ben rode shank's mare a substantial portion of the way from Edmonton to Vancouver, including an off-highway ramble between Revelstoke and Golden. He's seen so many rivers, lakes and tarns up high in the Rockies that sometimes it surprises him to see running water that's not cloudy with glacial silt. The stories he tells blend together in my memory, but I believe this summer was the year that he was spotted by a Fish and Wildlife official and written up as a sasquatch sighting.

Ben has promised to write us some posts for Kayak Yak about his times on the water in a variety of jury-rigged boats. He's also become a fan of the many ferries in BC, including a free car ferry on Kootenay Lake!

While he was here, Ben pulled on a wetsuit and borrowed one of my inflatable kayaks, the Expedition that I took down the Red Deer River last summer. (Yes, I'm still talking about that trip. When you paddle down a river solo, even a class 1 river, you get to talk about your trip too. And of course I'm still talking about the kayak cuz it's an incredible and portable boat!) I got into the littler inflatable and we went along the shoreline, around Flower Island and back. Shall have to write more about that day and the mink & otters we saw... And now he's back on the road again. Elvis has left the building.

FOGTOBER AND THE SEA Star Epidemic

Yep, we had a good Fogust and September, even with some rain spells. Now we're half-past Fogtober, and all the trees around the shorelines have been changing colours. Marvelous!

The last few days I've been on the water only a couple of times, six days apart. Augh! Withdrawal is tough, so I guess I am indeed hooked on kayaking. It's been foggy and breezy all that time, with an inversion holding foggy weather along the coast.

The payoff for foggy weather is that the fish come up to the surface, and otters come out to catch them. There was a family of otters out in Cadboro Bay on the weekend, blithely and lithely slithering around a school of fish. The otter's round heads bobbed in the smooth water that was barely wrinkled. When their tails flickered for a dive, the little splash showed for hundreds of yards (metres). It's great to paddle a quiet boat, quieter and slower than the zodiacs and motorboats that zoom around the little training yachts sailing in the bay.

I was glad to be on the water again. Lately, I've been jealous of the Gecko Paddlers and their casual outings to Race Rocks... but then, last week at a meeting with other university people studying digital humanities, a tenure-track professor looked enviously at me because last year I paddled down the Red Deer river, solo river camping. So, envy is a relative thing. I'll just go kayaking when and where I can, and let envy be a good servant rather than a poor master, eh?

And meanwhile, it's time for paddlers in the Salish Sea area to go out and look for sea stars. Check on the health of the starfish in your home waters, folks. The sea stars in Howe Sound seem to be suffering from some disease.

Not all sea star types are affected, as the leather and bat and blood stars seem to be doing well. The large sunflower sea stars are particularly badly affected. Instead of looking plump and full-fleshed, the sick starfish are emaciated. If you see sea stars looking like the one in this photo, or just decaying on the sea bottom, leave a comment on Vancouver Aquarium's website. Photos are helpful! Biologists trying to take affected animals for tests are appalled to find nothing but a bucket of goo by the time they get a sick starfish to the laboratory Divers are also looking in Saanich Inlet to see if there are similar problems here across the strait.

Areas in the Salish Sea have been affected by high populations of sea stars and sea urchins over the last several years, to the point where entire kelp forests are being eaten. I wonder if river otters and sea otters will be able to find plenty of urchins to eat, and thus maintain the kelp forests that sustain diverse shoreline life.

Waiatt and Rescues

T here was a rescue in Cadboro Bay one Sunday afternoon!

Sirens howled through the windy afternoon, as a firetruck rumbled down Sinclair Road into the parking lot of Gyro Park. Bernie and I found our shoes and followed our neighbour Curtis down to walk along the promenade and find out what all the sirens were for. A fire engine with ladder was there, as were two police cars.

And out in the bay, only about 200 yards offshore, was a small sailboat, belly-up. A person was hanging onto the hull, trying to right the boat. Black-clad, he appeared to be wearing a full-length wetsuit. There was a steady wind of over 25 km/hr and whitecap waves about 15 cm high.

Just as it became apparent that the cluster of firefighters and cops standing onshore were ineffective with their goodwill and telekinesis, a rescue boat roared across the bay. The Royal Victoria Yacht Club keeps a zodiac ready for just such events.

The people in the zodiac assisted the stricken boater with righting the sailboat and getting the spinnaker in place. The zodiac shepherded the sailboat back to the Yacht club, taking about three times as long as usual for the short hop.

This good news rescue is a great reminder for all of us to wear proper gear for immersion. Sunday's wind rose pretty suddenly. And we should keep in mind that it's not only our own cell phones or SPOT beacons or radios that will be used to call for rescue when it's really needed. There are often observers on shore who may or may not call 911.

Calling for rescue can be good news, as on this occasion where assistance was needed or else the boater was going to have to swim for shore and risk getting his sailboat wrecked.

It can also be embarrassing, as on the summer afternoon last year when a neighbour powered up his Pungo motorboat and cruised across Cadboro Bay to offer our paddle group a rescue. We had to admit that no, we were just having a practice session rehearsing our wet exits and recoveries... we weren't in distress. But thank you! And thank goodness this Good Samaritan hadn't called emergency services.

KAYAK MARTIAL ARTS

It was a marvellous morning when I tromped down to Gyro Park beach in Cadboro Bay, with my little inflatable kayak on my shoulder. You know the one... an old version of what's now the Lagoon. There are heaps of photos of it all over the Kayak Yak.

And as I passed the parking lot, two large dogs leapt out from a large car and began sniffing all around the grass and a pole and then noticed me. And my kayak. And did a double-take.

Well, you have to think of the meeting from their point of view. I was carrying the kayak on my shoulder, on the side facing them. To the dogs, I must have looked like some weird monster, perhaps in the shape of the Canadian National Film Board symbol (a giant eye with legs). The scent wouldn't have helped them, as to a dog it was a mix of PVC rubbery boat and a shortie neoprene wetsuit that no longer freshens up when washed with Mirazyme. Gah, a weird rubbery sweaty monster that swayed around! I may even have grunted as my sandal slipped in the mud.

No wonder they barked. No wonder they flinched back on their haunches and cowered, then advanced two steps. No wonder they growled and barked in the way that signals "Get back or I'll bite! I'm going to bite you NOW!"

The monkey that lives in the back of my head had that kayak off my shoulder in an instant. (You know that monkey... we all have one. It's pretty quiet most of the time.) I held the kayak between me and the dogs in a grip that couldn't have been improved: fingers around the paddle that was velcro'ed to the side of the deck, thumbs inside the cockpit pressing the inflated coaming against the paddle. I presented the smooth grey oval of the kayak hull to the advancing dogs. If those dogs bit, all they'd get would be a mouthful of PVC hull. And after shuffling that kayak across barnacled rocks, I was quite willing to let both dogs chew on it if necessary.

Did I mention that they were a German shepherd cross and a Blue Heeler? Strong, aggressive things that put together weighed as much as me?

But even as the monkey in the back of my head invented Kayak Martial Arts and put me into a Kung Fu stance, the frontal lobes were talking to the dogs. "Sit! Cut that out! I'm a person. Haven't you ever seen a boat? Come and smell it."

Their owner came up then, apologizing and admitting that the one dog was a rescue and had never seen a boat before. We did a quick session of introducing the dog to the boat and by our conversation showing her that the world did in fact include smelly boat-rubber people and their toys.

Then I went off and paddled on calm waters, spying baby otters and great blue herons and having a lovely time. Un-bitten. And apparently, a natural at Kayak Martial Arts.

WAIATT BAY, QUADRA Island

This summer, I got the chance to do something really special. As a volunteer assistant, I joined a biology project. A friend of mine in Straitwatch passed on an appeal from her friend Amy for volunteers to stay at an isolated campsite on Quadra Island, and take samples from beaches. Paddling skills would be an asset.

I joined three other volunteers and Amy for five days on the shores of Waiatt Bay. All these photos were taken by Amy Groesbeck, earlier this summer at similar trips. You won't see any photos of me in this post. You wouldn't want to. The day before the trip, I went to the dermatologist and had eight pink fleshy moles burned off my face with liquid nitrogen. Yuck. A good week to be out in the middle of the woods and the sea, away from most people. It was a good time – I got on the water every day in small boats, usually twice a day, and paddled miles of unfamiliar shorelines.

There's an app for that

Our transportation from Heriot Bay to Waiatt Bay at the north end of Quadra Island was on a boat called the *Gung Ho*, skippered by Harper Graham. He has a sensible manner that makes passengers feel confident that he knows where he's going and what he's got to do to get there. Of course he knows! On the dashboard in his wheelhouse, next to the throttle controls for the boat's engine and a GPS locator, lies an iPhone in its rubbery case. Yup, an iPhone. He took a text message or two before we finished motoring out of Heriot Bay. He also opened up an app or two and swiped at the phone's screen as he approached the islets in the bay. Perfect navigation. There's an app for that, apparently.

The bay is sheltered with several small islands that make up Octopus Islands Marine Park. Though it's only an hour away from Heriot Bay, Waiatt feels really isolated. That's partly because there's only one cabin visible along the shore, and partly because the second-growth timber has gotten pretty thick so the logging clear-cuts are all grown back in.

The place we camped is on the north shore of Waiatt Bay at the place the chart calls "Log Dump." This little cove has a stream running into the bay, and a midden where we camped, all thoroughly stomped on by the logging done here. Two old sheds and a camper are all falling to pieces in the trees.

All I have is a red canoe, three paddles and the truth(with apologies to U2 and Bono)

The skills to handle small boats are practical skills, with real-life applications for modern work in the sciences. One field that puts canoes and kayaks to serious use is... intertidal biology! At least, it does here on the wet coast.

We set out with two ancient canoes – one green, one red – and my little inflatable kayak. The photo Amy took shows a dark green boat she used on an earlier trip this summer. The canoes were laden with highly technical scientific sampling equipment. That's 5-gallon plastic pails, garden trowels, rubber-palmed garden gloves, spiral-bound notebooks and Zip-Loc freezer bags.

Okay, Amy had a transit of some kind with a laser level, too. She also had some squares she made, 25 cm on a side made out of 1-inch PVC tubing, so we could dig holes exactly 25 cm across. We had to dig them 30 cm deep, which is exactly the length from my elbow to my knuckles. I love the precision of scientific work! In a few beaches, there were experiments placed where Amy buried hand-made mesh bags holding living clams.

Oh, and I was also trained in how to make a sampling device. A kitchen scrubber called a Tuffy was attached to a ten-inch piece of rebar with a cable tie. Easy as pie. After the rebar was pounded into a clam garden, the Tuffy would sit there for four days, collecting anonymous sludge and (with any luck) clam spat. Apparently, intertidal biologists have been trying to figure out how to collect clam spat, and inventing various devices. Someone lucked into using kitchen scrubbers, and found that the Tuffy brand was particularly effective. Did I mention that this project had some funding from grants? Your tax dollars at work, and very efficiently, too. Why waste a biologist's time hand-knitting spat collecting filters when an affordable commercial alternative is easily available. The fun part is pounding the rebar into the garden, when the pounding has to be done underwater. Smack! Smack! into the water. "Science! Doing it all for science!" Spit out muddy sea water. "I'm still having fun!"

Dunno what YOU did on your vacation, but I sat on muddy beaches, dug holes, and collected clam spat. I didn't even ask if spat was gametes or zygotes. I wasn't the one picking up the Tuffy scrubbers and putting them in Zip-Loc freezer bags, and I didn't really need to know.

Nature's Art

On one island owned by a family that Amy knows, there's a cabin, hidden in the trees. It's decorated with all kinds of handmade art objects, made from wood and beach materials and boating materials. Visitors to the bay have been bringing their art objects here for years! When we got back to our camp at the log dump site, I took out my knitting and made a sweater. A little one, doll-size. The next day, we found a piece of driftwood and made a little person to put in the art cabin.

All in all they're just another rock in the wall

If you look over a clam garden at high tide, whether from a boat or from the shore, you probably wouldn't see anything to tell you that this is a place shaped by human gardeners.

When the tide is a little lower than full, you might guess at the shallows near shore, usually in a small bay or between two rocky points. But when the tide is low, approaching a zero tide, the clam garden is revealed.

From shore it looks like a flat, almost level shallow beach. It's mostly free of rocks bigger than your head. Most of the beach is sediments mixed with small stones and bits of broken clam shell. The clam shell hash was added deliberately, to change the local pH of the water and send chemical messages to floating clam spat that here was some good clam habitat to settle down and grow! At the edge of the garden is a rocky ledge. Most of these ledges don't stand up much higher than the level of the beach, maybe ankle-high. But if you look past the edge of the ledge, you can see that the sea bottom drops down suddenly. You're standing at the top of a wall made of rocks piled on rocks.

One of these walls can be as high as three or four metres or more above its underwater base. Most of the visible rocks look small enough for one person to have rolled down the beach into place, about twenty to thirty centimetres across. The rocks at the bottom of the wall three or four metres or more underwater may be larger, maybe half a metre across or bigger.

But that's really enough talking that I can do about clam gardens. To learn more about them, check out the totally awesome book *Clam Gardens*, by Judith Williams. You can read more about it at the website for the publisher New Star Books.

A bird in the hand is worth a snake in the shallows

We got to see lots of wildlife, around the shores of Waiatt Bay. My little kayak is so quiet that I could sneak up on these animals, shyer than their city cousins in Cadboro Bay. A few seals swam by to check out our boats. Raccoons like clam gardens! A couple of times we saw two or three raccoons waddling over the flats at low tide, digging for clams and various invertebrates. A mink poked out its head from the shoreline bushes to look at the canoes that had just gone by, then stare at me and squeak "oh crap!" before darting away. And right in our camp, a little brown weasel came scampering by and glared at everyone. For birds, there were ravens watching our every move, as well as kingfishers and a hummingbird, and a large eagle. I'm sure that we all were very glad that no black bears or cougars came by for a visit.

The most striking animal sighting was when Sara squeaked while sitting on a rocky ledge one afternoon. "A snake!" she squawked. A garter snake was sunning itself on the ledge beside her. When it slithered into the lukewarm sea water, our overjoyed amateur naturalists joined the actual biologists. A snake that swam in sea water! oooOOOoo!

Well, maybe the most striking animal was the polychaete, a bristly marine worm that snaked out of a tunnel in the side of the sampling hole that Sara was digging. Another squawk announced her shock at the arrival of the sandworm. This probably wasn't the kind of polychaete that the Kayak Yak paddle group found in Portage Inlet, making jelly ball egg sacs. That worm, according to Dr Kelly Sendal, probably looks rather like a bratwurst. This one in Sara's gloved hands looked more like a giant pink earthworm with tiny millipede legs. She carefully put it aside and went back to digging. And found another one in her next hole. Only a tiny squawk that time. Tough gal!

I love your lab!

The first time we catalogued clams, both living clams and the shells of dead clams, our group gathered under the tarp over our kitchen area. Seated on five-gallon pails, we hunched over our shells. Annemarie sorted shells, Amy and Kim measured shells with calipers, Sarah and I recorded the measurements in Amy's notebooks. Plenty of banter. "Clam me," I said. "All Clams, All Dead." A rain squall fell around us, and we got chilled and stiff before we were done and dinner could be made.

The second time was much more idyllic. That afternoon was sunny, so after lunch on a rocky slope below a midden across the bay from camp, we set up the calipers and notebooks. Each of us moved into the shade or sunshine at will by shifting a couple of feet on the moss. Our postures were not hunched this time, but varied from leaning on one elbow like a diner at a Roman feast to laying back against rocky slopes perfectly designed to support our backs and heads. More banter, as living clams were found among the dead samples and a dead clam among the living samples. Zombie clams don't groan "braiiinnzz", we decided, because they don't have brains. They call out for nerves.

Looking out across the bay was wonderful. I'd always thought that doing science involved wearing lab coats, not bathing suits or my shortie wetsuit. This place was much nicer than a basement lab somewhere. "I love what you've done with your lab!"

In an Octopus's Garden

We came to a clam garden one day that had an unusual living thing at the edge of a particularly high wall. It looked rather like a dahlia flower made out of yellowish jellyfish. "What the heck is that?" Amy wondered out loud. "A squid's egg sac?"

"Or an octopus's egg sac?" I suggested. "There are supposedly a lot of octopus around here. This is Octopus Islands Marine Park, after all." That didn't seem likely. Octopus mothers usually put their egg sacs in sheltered places, and protect them till the little ones hatch. But I found photos online of octopus egg sacs that look pretty much like what we saw.

We got to work taking samples, and Amy wrote notes in her books. When she asked "What shall we call this beach?" there was really only one name to consider: Octopus's Garden.

Here Comes The Rain Again

The weather was almost perfect – very little breeze on the water the second day, and a half-hour rain squall were the only variations from sunny and mild. In this sheltered bay the ocean water gets about as warm as it does anywhere along the coast, so it felt much warmer than where I usually paddle near Victoria. There were some two dozen sailboats anchored in sheltered places around Waiatt Bay, the most crowded that Amy had ever seen this area. Nights were cool but not really cold. And just in case perfect was asking too much, an hour before the *Gung Ho* returned to take us back to Heriot Bay, the clouds opened up. All our tents were soaked as we stuffed them into their bags. But it was still fun! And I got to do it again a few summers later.

MORE THAN I NEEDED to know about barnacles

Yes, I got out on the water this weekend. Nothing unusual, just a nice ordinary summer afternoon on the water. Instead of writing about that, though, I thought this was a chance to mention barnacles.

Barnacles are the bane of a fine kayak's existence. Well, maybe not the bane, but they're a danger to a fine finish on a kayak, anyway. Well, they are if the kayaker makes a habit of paddling along shorelines and in rock gardens.

And I do. My Eliza kayak from Necky has left skinny curls of pink plastic on barnacled rocks pretty much everywhere we go.

I can remember the first time John took his new blue Delta 14 kayak along the shoreline between Telegraph Bay and Gordon Head... He paused to take a photo of an eagle and got a little distracted. Sure enough, his kayak drifted over a rock that hid just under the surface of the water. The boomer had a couple of barnacles on it, and one scratched a line that went an embarrassing distance along the hull. Two years later, he sold that kayak, but a month later I spotted it on someone else's car roof rack. You know how I recognised it... yup, by that light but distinctive scratch.

Yeah, yeah, it's not the barnacles' fault. Those immobile little arthropods don't leap up and actively scratch my boat. If I kept a better eye on the rocks, there'd be no problem at all. So I decided to learn more about barnacles, since there are a lot of them in places I like to go. And besides, they look kind of neat when the tide comes in and all their feathery little feet come out to reach around, looking for food.

Something came to mind that biologist Amy Groesbeck told me when we were taking a clam sample in Waiatt Bay this summer. A researcher at Bamfield Marine Research Station has been learning things about barnacles that most of us will never get to see. Apparently, while barnacles are all hermaphrodites, their male equipment is more than one would expect, based on their body size. And adaptable to wave conditions. They're one of the few immobile species that has to couple, and well, that's about as far as I can take this story.

But don't let it end there. Check out videos on the internet, showing a romantic barnacle interlude.

WHALE!

Yes, I saw a whale! Yes, from a kayak, not from a zodiac with the Straitwatch biologist listening to the VHF radio to hear where whales had been sighted. I just went out and happened to see a whale.

When I put the kayak on my shoulder Thursday morning, I was just heading out for another mid-day paddle in my home waters. Same old same old, out to Flower Island and back. It was a pretty good moment for an ordinary outing, I gotta say. Clear blue sky, warm but not hot, no wind. Tide was out and heading lower.

By the time I got to Stein Island, the whale-watching boats were roaring in with roostertails of wake flaring behind them. Sonofagun. They were stopping right off Flower.

There's been this gray whale hanging around the Oak Bay area. The Times-Colonist newspaper wrote about people spotting it from Ten Mile Point to Trial Islands over the last two weeks. If you have no idea what a gray whale is, it's a good idea to do an online search for videos. A biologist was interviewed on local television, saying this whale looks young and healthy. There are YouTube videos of gray whales in Oak Bay harbour, which show what you might see from shore or a whale-watching boat.

This day, there were eight whale-watching boats in all, floating between Cadboro Point and Jemmy Jones Island, off Smuggler's Cove. They turned off their engines like good, conscientious nature watchers.

Mama Seal was floating in the little channel between Flower Island and Evans Rock. She glared at me, as if to say "You humans are WAY too noisy today!" I pulled up against the steep rocky shore of Flower, looking at the whale-watching boats to see if they knew where the whale was. I pulled into first one nook and then another. Tucked in among the rocks like this, inside the kelp at low tide, I was in barely enough water to float my kayak. The flexible, tough bottom of my boat rasped on the rocks and barnacles, but I didn't move offshore.

Gray whales feed in shallow water. Bernie has seen them right next to a cliff. Kathy saw this one just barely offshore at Turkey Head, browsing up food from the muddy shallow bottom. I was betting that the whale might even come between Flower and Evan. I had to be in a place that a whale absolutely couldn't need to go. These narrow rocky nooks wouldn't have stopped a transient orca hunting a seal, but a gray wouldn't want to roll on its tummy on a rock.

I heard it first. The whale came up to breathe, just off Evans Rock, and dipped down. Three breaths and a long pause under water, maybe six minutes or so.

The boats were really close – probably too close for the rules, but the whale seemed patient with us. I knew we were supposed to stay 100 metres away from a whale. But when the whale came closer than that, we boaters did the only thing we could: they shut down their motors and I huddled into the rocks.

Look on a map of Cadboro Bay there's Flower Island, off the big headland. See the rock just offshore? That's where I was, at low tide, tucked in with rocks all around and under my little inflatable kayak.

Yep, the good ol' Dragonfly, my reliable inflatable kayak from Advanced Elements. (The new version of this model is called the Lagoon, and it is even better.) Not the boat most whale-watchers use, admittedly. But that gray whale was getting followed rather too close for comfort, followed by four zodiacs and four big powerful howling boats full of whale-watchers. I was glad to be in something small and almost silent. And no other boat I have is both small and tough enough to sit on that wet rock shelf, just barely out of the whale's way. I am in awe of this kayak's outer shell. The material of the lower deck has some new scratches on it from today's adventure, as I shuffled my butt across a couple of barnacled rocks. The scratches are barely deep enough to see and feel – mere cosmetic damage.

The whale appears to have a few scrapes on its back, but no visible cuts or injuries. Apparently gray whales got that name from those mottled marks that look like scrapes or scars. And it's big! This is a young one? Good grief, how big are the mature ones? How big is this one compared to the really big whales? The sound of its breath is bigger and deeper than any animal I've heard, bigger than orcas and elephant seals. OMG.

SMARTCAR RELOADED

When the wheel broke off my luggage roller (the newer, larger roller, not the rusted smaller roller), it was a frustrating turn of events. It was not easy, dragging my inflatable kayak on one wheel and the corner of the roller frame. Commando kayaking was more of a battle that day than it usually is! Luckily, the Nature House was not an unreachable distance from the bus stop where the wheel broke.

But there was good news as well. When Marlene came to the lake to pick me up, we found that her SmartCar was big enough to hold the Expedition kayak. Hurray!

Some polite astonishment has been expressed, concerning the idea that the kayak in its bag would fit into the SmartCar fourtwo. Just astonishment, not disbelief. Those SmartCars are pretty small, after all.

Well, yeah, it is kinda hard to imagine shoehorning a 13-foot kayak into a fourtwo. As Louise suggested, photos are the only way to go. So here they are:

Thanks to Bernie's camera work, we have a series of images to show of Marlene's car being put to use. First of all, Bernie got a photo of the cargo bay behind the two seats, empty and ready for gear. He noticed particularly that the inside walls of the cargo area are black in the lower portion, and light grey in the upper portion.

Next, he got a picture of two inflatable kayaks loaded in the back of the SmartCar, just as Marlene figured they would fit. The yellow bag is smaller than the grey one, and she said to put it on top because the back of the car gets a little narrower as you go from bottom to top. But once both bags were in, we realised that we could have put two Expeditions in, easily. These bags hold the kayaks, folded, the safety gear, air pumps, and personal flotation devices (PFDs). The one four-piece paddle I own is tucked inside the yellow bag as well. I try to ignore the broken zipper on the grey bag.

Not only the boats but all the necessary gear must fit, for a successful trip. My small luggage roller tucked between the kayak bags so it won't roll around. We put a two-piece paddle on top of the bags, and a blanket rolled up beside them. A bungee cord got tucked down at the floor level. D'ya know how high the gear got piled? Not even shoulder-height on the driver! The driver could see right over all the gear.

In the passenger seat was my knapsack of gear (holding a change of clothes, lunch, a book, my knitting, and the laptop computer I'm currently writing on) that sat at my feet. It took up much less than half of the space for the passenger's feet, so I had plenty of room. There was also plenty of room in the front for Marlene's knapsack as well, and her jacket.

With the back closed on all that gear, there was still room to see out the back window. Not the entire window, but much of it. From the driver's seat the driver was able to see right over the yellow kayak bag through most of the window. Visibility really helps a driver feel better on the road! Marlene was still able to use her rearview mirror.

The final tally of gear loaded into the SmartCar that day:

1 13-foot Expedition kayak from AdvancedElements (the gold standard for inflatables, in my experience)

1 8'6" kayak from Advanced Elements (the Dragonfly, an older model of what's now the Lagoon)

1 two-piece paddle

1 four-piece paddle

2 PFDs with whistles, one with a compass, cold weather cap, and SPOT emergency device

2 water pumps

2 throw bags holding 50 feet of floating rope

2 air pumps (doublestroke pumps the size of my thigh, I might add)

1 folding luggage roller (and there was plenty of room for another)

2 knapsacks

2 jackets

1 blanket

1 SmartCar first aid kit

1 steel travel mug

1 bottle of water

I'll just add that there were two small purses in the knapsacks. Not sure what Marlene's purse held besides her wallet, key ring, phone, makeup and meds. Mine held all that plus an assortment of useful tools, eyeglasses, handkerchief, tissues, matches/lighter, candle, space blanket, granola bars, Purelle, pens and notepaper.

We were loaded for bear!

If this type of vehicle were regularly being used for this purpose, I would pack only one of the big air pumps plus a small one for a spare. I would also invest in two more paddles that take apart into three or four pieces, small enough to fit inside the kayak bags. The two-piece paddle was the only thing that took some wriggling to fit into the back of the car.

RESCUE

Soon as I got back into town, I put a quick note on Kayak Yak website, using my mother's computer. Now that my own computer is set up, I'll tell all y'all about the summer day that has put our rescue practices into actual practice. To sum up, two people rescued. No apparent injuries. Long description follows, for anyone who's interested.

Yesterday, the weather was great on Beaver Lake, the narrow end of a vaguely figure-8 shaped lake which we've written many blog posts about for Kayak Yak website, as we paddle there a lot. I was out in my little Dragonfly inflatable kayak (a 7-year-old model of what's now called Lagoon), and my friend Heather was rowing her inflatable rowboat (a Seahawk 2 rated as able to carry an adult and a child). These both are awesome little boats for commando kayaking, I should add – portable, stable, easy to set up, and way way tougher than the cheap little pool toys sold for ten bucks in chain stores. It's easy as pie to carry these boats on the bus and get them to the shore. Turns out, they're reasonable for rescuing tired swimmers, as we were very careful...

It was Saanich's Strawberry Festival, and big crowds were at Beaver Beach but the lake had few people in it or on it. After enjoying strawberries and ice cream, we had a lovely chat with a fireman (Emergency Services had some booths set up and a Command Centre in a big white RV). Then Heather and I set up our boats and launched. Our little debate about whether to bring her old-style PFD or a seat cushion resolved with her sitting on the cushion. Wonderful how safety equipment can also make us more comfortable – in this case, by boosting her up out of the usual wet-foot puddle in the bottom of her boat. It was 3:15 before we got on the water.

After some relaxed drifting and chatting, Heather said suddenly, "What's that red thing in the water?" We paddled closer to an island to investigate what turned out to be someone's red t-shirt. Someone was swimming among the weeds around the bushy shoreline of the island. He called hello, and asked for a tow.

That's how we met Rob: a young guy in his twenties, tired and tangled in weeds. He took hold of the stern of my kayak and let me tow him out to clear water. There we re-assessed his situation. He was looking for the red canoe he and his dad brought to the island, with a six-pack of beer and a bottle of vodka. Could we please tow him around the island to look for the canoe? He was just too tired to swim through the weeds any more, and his backpack was getting heavy.

"Oh! You have a nice big boat!" he said to Heather. "I'll just get in and ride." He let go of my boat and grabbed for hers. There were weeds wrapped all around his legs and an arm. When we warned him not to flip us, he didn't inspire us with confidence that he could follow orders. It was hard enough for him to take off his backpack when we said so, because it was holding him down in the water. "Man, my electronics are all gonna be soaked," he said unhappily.

Meanwhile, Heather tied her float rope to her seat cushion. With that floating support, Rob was much happier; and with him floating ten feet away, we were much happier. After several tries, I rolled his insanely-heavy pack onto my front deck. There had to be 15 or 20 litres of water in that pack, so I began draining some of the water out through a partly-opened zipper. Peeking in, I saw shoes, jeans, and a plastic bag. Oh yeah, he had soaked whatever phone or camera was in here.

Was it time to push the emergency button on my SPOT beacon and call for rescue? Not quite, we decided. Rob could still talk coherently, and held on to his floating cushion fine. Warm day, good weather, and a beach on the lakeshore closer than whatever rock on the other side of the island where his dad and/or red canoe might or might not be, with whatever was left of the beer and vodka.

"Let's get him to shore," said Heather, tying the tow rope to my kayak's stern handle.

"You go ahead," I told her, "And get that nice young man we talked to with the big white truck." She nodded, realizing that if we said the words Emergency Services, Rob might get all upset at the notion of us calling the cops on him. Then he'd be even harder to deal with. Heather rowed to Beaver Beach, while I paddled to North Beach with Rob twenty feet behind me.

(Just for the record, if we hadn't known Emergency Services people were at the beach, we would have sent the emergency signal on the SPOT at that moment, and still begun towing him to shore.)

Rob chatted much of the way to the lakeshore, repeating what he said earlier. Towing a tired swimmer is much harder than towing a friend while playing or safety practise! Rob was doing an excellent imitation of a sea anchor.

Meanwhile, Heather had reached the shore only to find that the Emergency Services people had left. (We learned later that day that they were called out to another problem with some kids at another lake.) She borrowed a phone to call 911. Then she rowed back to the island, where she couldn't see the canoe but could hear Rob's father shouting for him. Good enough! He could stay there for now.

I pushed the OK button to celebrate when I got to shore. Rob staggered ashore and shook my hand. He sat at a picnic table, pulled his jeans and shoes out of his pack, and eventually struggled into them. "It's gonna take me an hour and a half to walk home," he said, and off he went. He wouldn't wait for his dad. Heather met me at North Beach, and we traded stories.

Heather and I went back to Beaver Beach, where a police car was pulled up on the grass close to shore nearly an hour and a half after the 911 call. Officer Brad needed some explanations, and used his radio to tell Fire Rescue to get a boat on the lake to pick up Rob's father. Brad set off to meet them at the Elk Lake end of the lake, and asked us to hang around in case Fire Rescue came to launch here instead. Meanwhile, Heather and I unlocked the Nature Centre. Never been so glad to have the key to that little building!

We folded up our boats, replaced various soggy clothes with dry, and re-fueled with cookies and water. We called my mom for a ride. Just before she got there, Officer Brad came back to tell us that Rob had been found walking along the road. And his father had been found in Elk Lake with a canoe part-way to shore and been rescued because he tipped over just as the Fire Rescue boat reached him. It was 6:45pm.

All in all, a good reminder of why we make such an issue about safety here on the blog – safety in so many ways:

-the importance of sturdy boats instead of cheap and flimsy pool toys

-familiarity with boat and gear

-experience in various conditions

-safety gear (rope, flotation device, and dunk bag were all put to use)

-safety practise (Heather and I had practised towing in various configurations many times)

-general first aid (doesn't matter much whether someone is impaired by fatigue, a bump on the head, or alcohol if that impaired someone flips your boat and grabs your head – to avoid that flip, it's much more important to figure out whether that someone is a little impaired or a lot!)

-safe drinking (both Heather and I were dehydrated by the end of our afternoon's adventure – and I'm wondering if alcohol was a factor in Rob's behavior)

What should we have done differently? In retrospect, since the tired swimmer needed to be towed to shore and his father needed to be found, calling 911 was the right thing to do. The only difference is that we should have used the SPOT emergency signal instead of having one of us paddle to the emergency guys at the beach. The rescue of Rob's father might have been put in motion earlier.

Horne Lake and Toronto

F riday was an excellent day for paddling! I hadn't been out on the water for three weeks, and missed it. The Eliza was gliding smoothly when I launched at Cadboro Bay. I've paddled here so many times in the last few years, and this time was much like the others. Bright overcast, not too cloudy. Low tide, coming in over familiar rocks. But sometimes something special happens in the middle of all the ordinary places and weather.

I didn't try to set any speed records, just drifted along looking at rocks covered with seaweed and various things, mostly squishy. Found a plotch of sea pork, which is a bit like a sea sponge but the colour of pink meat and clings to rocks. Saw a crab different from any I'd seen before, bluish, with long thin legs but not a spider crab. And a metre away from it was another, a little smaller. Go crabs go! There's a boat comes through the bay almost every week setting out crab traps. The crabs need every chance they can get. And I saw a little sea star, the sunstar kind with over a dozen arms, that was only the size of my hand. The tube-feet reached out as it wriggled a couple tentacle arms slowly, perhaps looking for water.

I drifted from Flower Island to the rocks near it that we call "Whale Rock" because at high tide it looks like a whale under your boat. Then I saw a familiar motion, as a family of otters came climbing down from the brush on Flower Island.

There were at least eight of them, maybe nine, all sleek and plump and limber. And for sure, river otters are colour-blind, because I sat there in my bright pink kayak, wearing an orange PFD and a red-and-black hat, holding a paddle with yellow blades. They swam close to where I was drifting, and began ducking down into the shallows. Every few moments one or another would surface with something in its paws or jaws, and chew away. They looked busy and happy.

Eventually one poked up its head and took a good, long look in my direction. I'm guessing that pattern recognition finally told them that I was there.

They squeaked, ducked, and swam a few yards farther away, no more. Even so, I took this as my cue to leave. No point putting pressure on them and making them feel crowded. I headed back toward the beach at Gyro Park.

And on the way, there was another pair of otters at the little rock garden, fishing there with a heron nearby. There's wonderful things *everywhere* in spring!

VISITING TORONTO

Time to post a trip report! Well, a trip report in progress at least, while I was in the Toronto area for two weeks, doing a pair of readings for the Toronto Public Library's Heritage Reading Series. (Sorry, I haven't put a hot link here. But google Toronto Public Library and Heritage Reading Series and go check out their great website! A page for each reading, including location of the library branch it's in, and transit info for how to get there.)

This was a welcome visit to the metro Toronto region, as I hadn't seen Bernie's niece and nephew for almost three years. They got bigger for some reason...

I brought my Dragonfly kayak on the plane, which got me only a few comments from the other passengers when I put it in the overhead compartment. No, really, I checked it as baggage and it travelled fine, even with a two-part paddle sticking out of one end of the zipper. Bernie's sister was pleased to see the kayak bag fit fine into the trunk of her car. It also fit fine on the landing of the basement stairs at her family home in Mississauga near the airport. Or it did until her husband got tired of walking past it and carried the bag the rest of the way downstairs and out of the way in the basement.

Once he went to work the next day, it wasn't too hard for me to wrestle the bag through the basement and upstairs. I trundled it along the sidewalk and onto a transit bus with a small dolly, and transferred twice on my way to the Credit River where it empties into Lake Ontario. Other paddlers on the quiet river today reminded me not to go out into the Great Lake, as a breeze on the river can pick up some big waves out on the open water. I think they had no idea what kind of waves I've paddled in, but they meant the advice well, and as it happens I stayed on the river.

I caught the #8 S bus to the Don Rowing Club and the Mississauga Canoe & Kayak Club. Three ol' boys at the rowing club let me change clothes in the ladies' room, and I set up my inflatable behind the canoe club. Though I'd e-mailed ahead, there was no one at the Canoe & Kayak Club at 10:30 am on a Friday morning. I launched from their steep ramp and set out on the quiet flatwater. It felt a lot like any river estuary, but there was no salt in the spray or wind, of course!

The river is only about 200 metres across at its mouth, between a recreation centre and a dolled-up lighthouse. There's a yacht club outside the mouth, and the two small boating clubs just upriver from the bridge for Lakeshore Drive and downriver from the trestle for the GO train to Toronto.

I paddled under the low trestle, passing Canada geese, a swan, mallard ducks, swallows, red-wing blackbirds, some black-and-white woodpeckers and a kingfisher, as well as something that looked like a Caspian tern but was probably more common. Some large bird soared overhead but I couldn't tell if it was an eagle or something else.

The river at this point is a muddy, grey-green khaki colour, but there are no industrial buildings on either side, just a lot of *very expensive* houses. The variety of steps down to the water from the houses on the bluffs is really interesting... some steps and docks are obviously homestyle constructions, most are rather well-made and look like they'd be good for backyard/beach parties. The trees on either side are almost all deciduous and had just dressed themselves in new leaves. Very fresh looking and smelling! The river didn't stink, but it certainly wasn't pristine wilderness.

I made easy headway upriver, as there was very little current (maybe 1/2 knot) and the breeze was blowing upstream. It only took about half an hour to pass under the bridge for the Queen Elizabeth Parkway.

At one point I found another inflatable kayaker, who proudly announced he'd just camped the night on the sandbar island he'd just left. There were a lot of low bushes and scrubby willow trees on the sandbar islands, so it was easy to see how he could hide a small tent or something. That's where I also saw a turtle basking on a log, neck and legs extended in the thin sunshine. It looked like a red-eared slider, grown big enough not to have a red patch any more.

At some points, there were no houses visible from the water; at others, very few and only partly visible through trees. All in all, a pleasant urban waterway, very park-like even when not actually parkland.

Up-river from the QE there's a golf course, and there the current picked up as the river became more shallow. I worked my way upstream for a while, but eventually turned round and let the little current (about 2 knots) carry me back down to quieter waters.

There yet another inflatable kayaker praised the merits of a boat that he can store in his condo, and pointed out a muskrat swimming across the river.

I was on the water for over two hours in a slow, easy flatwater paddle, and wished I'd been able to go farther upstream. Another time, I'll try to borrow a kayak from someone at the club and go up by the golf courses.

Next time – the Toronto Islands! And I get to fulfill my fantasy of portaging my boat on a Toronto subway.

TORONTO ISLANDS

On my second outing of commando kayaking in Metro Toronto, I wrestled my inflatable kayak into my sister-in-law's car trunk. She dropped me at Square One in Mississauga, and I hopped onto the GO bus to Union Station, downtown Toronto.

Once there, I trundled the kayak into the station, down stairs, and onto a streetcar to the waterfront. It was a four-block walk, with Bay Street to cross, so the streetcar was a good alternative. Then onto the little ferry to the Toronto Islands.

When Bernie was here, he rented a plastic kayak from a place on Harbourfront and paddled across the harbour. I was paddling the Dragonfly model inflatable and there was a lot of traffic in the harbour that morning, so it seemed sensible to take the ferry to the little islands. Sure enough, there were several sailboats out for their first bright day of the summer.

It was a bright day, from time to time, and just a little breeze to start that picked up as the day went on. I hopped off the ferry at Hanlan's Island, changed in the restroom, and puffed up the boat. Strapping everything on the deck was a little tricky, as it raised the centre of gravity, but the Dragonfly is a pretty stable ride. Putting anything under my seat was NOT on, as it raised MY centre of gravity high enough to mess with my muscle sense of balance.

Hanlan's Island is a nice place, less crowded than the rest of the islands. I saw many birds during the day, including a scarlet tanager and a kingfisher and something like a great blue heron with a short neck.

Five different tour boats cruised past me at intervals during the day. Lots of little power boats at marinas in these islands, and many houses on Ward's Island or Algonquin Island have boats and decks at the shoreline.

I made my way slowly around Centre Island to Ward's Island and got out at the ferry terminal there. note to self: launch and land on the east side of the terminal, not the west side as I did.

All in all, it was three and a half hours of paddling in quiet, sheltered waters (except when I rounded two islands, and that was still on the harbour side). I'll do it again someday, and hope to have friends along.

Humber River in Etobicoke

THE THIRD TIME'S THE charm! Taking a kayak out for a single paddle might have been just a whim, but taking it on a plane trip and using it three times apparently makes me a hardcore kayaker. At least, my sister-in-law thinks I am. And that's really what counts.

This outing, my kayak was still in downtown Toronto after a gorgeous day paddling in the Toronto Islands (three hours and fourteen GLORIOUS nights). I had taken it back to the mainland on the ferry, then on the streetcar to the Merril Collection of Science Fiction in the Lillian Smith branch of Toronto Public Library. Lorna Toolis, librarian, let me leave the kayak in her office overnight, so I could go to a reading and a friend's house without schlepping it around.

In the morning, I returned to her office and traded my little daypack & walking stick for the kayak, then trundled it onto the streetcar and the Bloor-Yonge subway. Off at Old Mill station, up a *very* long flight of stairs.

A few days earlier, I had noticed this river valley under the station looked like a park and checked out some online listings that said it was a good paddling destination. The Humber River is indeed a good flatwater paddle, through King's Mill Park to Lake Ontario, by all reports.

It's only a block or two to the water from Old Mill station, all downhill. I found sufficient trees at the riverbank to let me change into merino wool paddling gear (the weather was much too warm for neoprene!). This time I strapped all my gear onto the front deck and put the roller inside under my legs and it felt more balanced than the day before, when some gear was on the back deck.

The river was calm, and just as grey-green as the New Credit. I drifted downstream past the Humber River Yacht club, and made friends with a large swan who contested with several Canada geese for bread being scattered by a regular park visitor. So good to be the boat on the water, as cars went by on the bridge overhead, and subway trains roared past on their own bridge.

It wasn't a challenging paddle. But it was a relaxing one, with kingfishers and swallows swooping around, and just enough rain sprinkling to keep the whole outing quiet and private. Going upstream was no effort, and it was nice to see the houses on the high bluffs from the opposite angle now, and to follow the bends back to the old mill and the pedestrian stone bridge.

Went ashore, got changed and packed up with a family of geese staring at me warily.

I even towed the kayak uphill to the station without any problems, though I did make two cars swerve around me on the quiet residential street. A total of five people that day pointed at the kayak bag, and said, "Golfing?"

Nice to take a break from the big city skyscrapers, and just drift like that.

HONK

THE BEST STORY I CAN tell about a kayaking trip is the one about our trip to Horne Lake. For those of you who have never been there, I can advise you that the gravel road from the Island Highway was actually pretty good for the first several miles. The last mile to the campground, however, was awful. And the final half-mile of road to Horne Lake Provincial Park was truly dreadful, with deep ruts and potholes full of rainwater.

So it was a relief to set up our two tents and get out my Advanced Elements inflatable. My daughter got out her photography equipment, and my husband unloaded the newspaper, a book, and a pound of red licorice. We booked a tour in the Horne Lake Caves for the next morning. I paddled on Horne Lake that afternoon with great pleasure, going around the point from the campground.

It was a good day for paddling. I sent several OK messages with my SPOT device. I looked up at the great cliff above the lake, with bent layers of rock in big streaks. I checked out Little Qualicum River, where it was choked with fallen trees. Later in the day, the wind picked up a little, as could be expected. There was a long fetch along the biggest part of the lake. But I only had to work across the wind for part of the way back, and when I got back around the point the wind blew me along and back to the beach where I had launched.

Dinner was more than just red licorice. The best thing about camping on a kayaking trip is that you can bring a lot of tasty, nutritious, heavy food. We ate till we were stuffed, then put the rest of the food back in the car so that raccoons wouldn't come looking for it. We were all tired, and got into our sleeping bags early that evening.

We'd only been asleep for an hour when we learned the second best thing about camping on a kayaking trip – you can bring your camping gear in your kayak and camp out far away from other people. But we didn't do that this time: I was paddling out and back each day from the campground. We learned the worst thing about camping – it's when there are unwanted neighbours. These neighbours had been no problem all afternoon and evening. But at eleven o'clock that night, in a nearby campsite, someone's car alarm went off. Honk, went the horn. Honk. Honk.

We lay in our sleeping bags, waiting for the owner to turn off the alarm. After a while, my husband whispered, "Who the *hell* sets their *car alarm* on a *camping trip*?"

Honk. Honk. "Someone who doesn't want the raccoons to break in and steal their food?" I suggested, after several Honks. "Or someone who put something valuable in the car? Like our daughter put her camera equipment in the car."

"I *locked* the car," he said. "What good is a car alarm going to do?"

Honk. Honk. "Must have everybody in the campground awake," I guessed. "Ooo, somebody's going to be unpopular."

"Why the *hell* haven't they turned off the *alarm*?" he whispered.

Honk. Honk. "They're taking a long time to turn that alarm off," I said. "Maybe they can't find the keys."

"Don't *need* keys," he said. "Give me your pocket knife and a *rock*."

Honk. Honk. "Sh. You can't just break into someone's car and cut the wires," I said. Honk. Honk. "Not yet, anyway." Honk. Honk. "Maybe in a while." Honk. Honk. "We'd do it together, and talk so the neighbours know we're not stealing the car."

"All the neighbours are *certainly* awake," he agreed. Honk. Honk.

"Maybe the car owner is in Qualicum Beach, having a beer," I suggested. "Drove there with a friend." Honk. Honk. "Won't be back till later."

"He'd *better* be in town, having a beer," whispered my husband. "If he's sitting in his campsite *listening* to this racket, I'd *kill* him."

Honk. Honk. "I think you'd have a dozen witnesses to swear that he was hit by a meteor." Honk. Honk.

"And I'd have *help* throwing the body into the river," he whispered. Honk. Honk. Somehow the idea of stuffing the car's owner into one of the caves never got suggested aloud. Doing such a nasty thing to the perfectly nice caves seemed really wrong.

"Of course, you and the angry mob might run into a handyman with a toolbox and a cooler head, older and wiser, coming to cut the car's wires," I pointed out. Honk. Honk.

"A guy like that, he'd *know* what was going on," my husband said. Honk. Honk. "He'd figure it out at a *glance*." Honk. Honk. "*He'd* say, You're gonna want to make it look like an *accident*."

"He'd say, I've got a broken kayak paddle you can put with him. But no, they'll never believe the guy was kayaking in those clothes. I'll go get a fishing rod and some tackle and meet you lot by the river canyon." Honk. Honk.

"You know, I can *hear* you," our daughter said from inside her own little tent next to ours. "Don't say any more. I need *some* deniability. How am I supposed to be a plausible *alibi* for you?" Honk. Honk.

At that point we heard the sound of an ancient Datsun hatchback approaching, making its way along the potholed road. The evening chorus now went: Honk. Rrmmm. Sploosh! Honk. RrRmMmm. Sploosh! Honk. The car eventually came to a halt at a nearby campsite. We could clearly hear three big goons get out of the car, like clowns at a circus. They bumbled around for a few minutes, dropping things and running into each other, before managing to turn off the car alarm.

Blessed silence returned. Well, nearly silence. There was plenty of drunken shushing and giggling for a while. But we were already asleep.

Next morning, I was up and carrying my kayak to the water first thing. On the way, I could see a campsite with an ancient Datsun hatchback parked next to an SUV with three kayaks on the roof, and the hood up, and wires trailing from the engine.

MARLENE AND THE WHALE

Our friend Marlene envied our delight in our few sightings of whales. Not the sightings, but the delight. She had never had good experiences with whales; once in a fishing boat, an orca had approached and frightened her, but the people she was with hadn't been supportive. Several times throughout her life, she had nightmares about whales. Perhaps it was from her heritage. At any rate, going on salt water in a kayak with our paddling group was only possible if we could assure her this place was very unlikely to have a whale approach.

Then came the summer there were many stories of a young grey whale hanging around Oak Bay near Turkey Head. People at the marina or along the shoreline path were able to see the whale swimming nearby, and with binoculars they could clearly see the whale come up to breathe then duck down. That was when Marlene resolved to face her fear of whales, and asked us to show her this whale – from shore, not from a boat! If she was standing on shore, that should be okay, and she didn't expect to be too afraid. The whale would be in the sea where it belonged, and she would be on land where she belonged. It should be nothing like her nightmares.

So, Bernie and I and Marlene got into my dad's truck and we went to look for the whale. The weather was good in Oak Bay as we scanned the waves with binoculars. After half an hour, Marlene was cold in the offshore breeze, and wrapped up in my shawl. Then we noticed the whale was swimming several hundred metres away – we could see clouds of its breath when it came up, and the curve of its back as it dove. Over and over again, the whale rose and sank, and we were thrilled to see it.

At least, Bernie and I could see it. Maybe binoculars didn't work so well for Marlene. Certainly a dull grey curve of back in a dull grey sea was hard for her to find. "I can't see it very well," she said. "Won't it come any closer?" It was Bernie who suggested that she call the whale to come closer.

And she did.

She called to it quietly, asking for the whale to come closer, where we could see it better. She promised to stay on the shore and look at it, if the whale would please come close enough for her to see.

And it did.

The young whale came much closer, into the shallows, and seemed to relax even as we gasped in wonder. Marlene was trembling with cold, but her fear got less as she watched. The whale was so big, she said. Several times, it ducked down to feed on the sandy bottom, then rose to breathe, swimming past us, back and forth along the shore. Other people noticed, and pointed out the whale to each other as they stood quietly nearby with their cameras.

The whale moved to our left, and we followed at the same speed along the footpath above the shore, bringing a trail of admiring whale-watchers with us. The path came to a little rocky point, a breakwater sheltering the marina, where teenagers were balancing on their bicycles. When the teens saw Marlene, shawl fluttering, and the whale, they retreated to the footpath and the grass above it. Meanwhile, the whale nosed its way along the breakwater, clearly visible to admirers on the shore, and then approached us again along the other side, into the marina.

Astonishingly, the whale nosed its way between one dock of boats and the breakwater, right up to where Marlene stood. It turned majestically, and made its way back to the end of the breakwater, accompanied all the way by joyful cries of wonder and thanks and the clicking of cameras. As the whale swam away from shore towards the Chain islets offshore, the whale-watching tourists and locals thanked Marlene for calling the whale to be seen.

ROCKS!

This year, I missed the first day of Paddlefest in Ladysmith, BC. After five years, it was a disappointment not to be there to see all the boats lined up along the shore, and talk with other kayakers. But I missed the first day of the kayaking festival for something really good instead – something my paddling group has been looking for since we first paddled off Sidney, BC.

It was all for rocks.

One look shows how different the rocks are from one headland and island to another around Vancouver Island. There's something important to learn about geology here on the Saanich Peninsula. Look on Kayak Yak website at some of our kayaking group's photos from Robert's Bay and Coal Island and the Little Group! But how to learn the local rocks? Hands-on is the best way to learn in the physical sciences. We needed a tour with a geologist. And I got one on that Saturday in May.

The Capital Regional District of Greater Victoria set up the tour, finding a geologist from the Pacific Geoscience Centre on Patricia Bay near the airport. Dr Chris Yorath took two dozen of us volunteer naturalists off on a wild tour of several sites, from Island View Beach and Parker Park to Cattle Point, Finlayson Point, Goldstream River, Esquimalt Lagoon and then to Tower Point at Witty's Lagoon.

Most of these places I've been to lots of times as a child and an adult. Tower Point is a park that previously I've only seen from my kayak, when we're rounding Albert Head and going to Witty's Lagoon. You can see our blog posts on the website Kayak Yak about that area. Parker Park is a beach access that I hadn't used before, but around Victoria there are beach accesses everywhere. The municipality of Saanich had to explain to one developer that property fronting onto Portage Inlet couldn't just cut off public access to the beach. I love it that the government is on our side on the issue of beach access!

Walking along the shoreline at place after place, Yorath spoke about the ancient origins of several kinds of rock in this part of the world. As the continent of North America drifted westward for millions of years, it ran into island chains (something like Hawaii today) that piled up along the West Coast. All of British Columbia is made up of these wrinkled ridges of rock, previously separate but now smushed together, called terrenes. Several of these terrenes can be found packed together here at the south end of Vancouver Island. Even easier to see were the most recent geological changes, caused by the glaciers of the most recent Ice Age. Yorath showed us basalt pillows that originated in undersea volcanoes a hundred million years ago, and that have been carved away by glaciers. The rock underfoot has veins of quartz, tilted layers of shale, sandstone, sandy bluffs, and conglomerate.

Yorath is exactly the geologist you want for a tour like this! He literally wrote the book on local geology – *Geology of Southern Vancouver Island*, revised edition. While we were on the beach at Parker Park in Cordova Bay, we ran into students from Royal Roads University who carried copies of the book. Shyly, they asked for his autograph.

Yorath knows his earth science, and he has been walking over these local sites for decades. The man showed us his favourite basalt pillow. Any scientist with a favourite example of a rock formation is my kinda scholar! He spoke of how the scientists who studied mid-oceanic volcanic ridges were working locally, confirming not only the theory of continental drift but the reversals of the Earth's magnetic field. The places we walked over and examined were the ordinary parks we naturalists had visited for years, but with Yorath's commentary we understood them in new ways.

The rocks around us looked so permanent, but he showed us that we could see the changes and how one layer of rock overlay another. Fifty million year old rock actually looked newer than rock a hundred million years old. We could see the weathering and cracking in some places, and the big gouges from glaciers in others.

Yorath told us that the edge of the North American continent is colliding with and riding up over the Pacific Plate under the Pacific Ocean. Those mountains we could see across the Strait of Juan de Fuca, the Olympic Mountains in Washington State, were being forced higher and higher at an inch or a couple of centimetres a year. Wind and rain and gravity was wearing down those mountains too, at about the same rate, so the peaks wouldn't get much higher than they were now.

We could see why, for example, the Gulf Islands are mostly made of harder shale, where the softer sandstone has been worn away by water and glaciers. John has taken photos showing layers of shale along the west shore of Thetis Island. And now I understand why our beaches are a muddle of many kinds of stone – it's because the glaciers scraped across this whole area time and again. Bits of stone and sand clung to the bottom of the moving ice and were carried for a short way or for many miles from one terrene to another before being left behind as the ice melted. During the latest Ice Age, sea level had been over a hundred feet lower than it is now. Ten thousand years after the great glaciers melted, the land here is still rebounding, springing up now that the great weight of ice is gone.

During Yorath's career, the rocks hadn't changed except for the most minimal of weathering, but the understanding of geology had changed profoundly. It made me dizzy, to see these stones the way he spoke about them. Time was suddenly something to think about differently than the speed of my own movements. Hot lava emerged from underwater volcanoes, cooling quickly to glass on the outside curves of slowly hardening billows and pillows. Grit and organic debris settled down so thickly and for so long that it compacted into rock under its own weight and under new lava. Mountains split and piled up like the snow I plowed from my driveway. Smooth, flat shale and slate bent like taffy, pushed by a continent colliding with volcanoes sprung from an ocean floor. There's a big bend in the layered rock visible on a cliff above Horne Lake, up-Island, and I could see it twisting in my mind's eye, an inch a year. Rigid bedrock was springing up underfoot as the weight of the glaciers melted away ten thousand years ago. The slump at the south end of James Island, making a sandy bluff and shallows, fluttered like my hair in the offshore breeze. The ocean water around our islands was as transparent as the air to my new vision.

I felt like a mayfly, or a daylily, fluttering in my short, twittering life while glaciers ran like the rivers where I paddle my kayak and the limestone and sandstone silted up and hardened like the mud on my kayak and my shoes. It was humbling.

You can understand that I kind of staggered around for the next couple of days. I was observing things! I was walking into the deep past, and watching how rock hardened and layered and bent. It all felt as familiar as cooking jam and watching it set, or stretching taffy, or baking an impossible pie that settles out its own crust and topping. It especially felt like shovelling snow off the frozen driveway – the weight and the pressure and the texture changes. And of course, the rocks were familiar... they were the same ones I'd clambered over since I was a child.

ANOTHER PADDLEFEST

Paddlefest in Ladysmith again! It was great. Once again, several members of our paddling group insisted on attending. Well, we're not sure if Rich made it up on his own on Saturday. And Marlene had a bad case of "it's eight o'clock Sunday morning!" when it was time to head out. But John and Louise drove up on Saturday and had a great time. You can read about it in the post John wrote on Kayak Yak, and see his great photos.

Bernie and I drove up-Island to Ladysmith on Sunday. We missed the crowds and good weather on Saturday, because there was a geology tour offered to the volunteer naturalists by CRD Parks. There were still good times on Sunday at Paddlefest, though the intermittent rain thinned the crowd to true believers.

As Brian Henry of Ocean River sports store said, most of the people attending on Sunday were confirmed kayakers. We need to find a way to encourage people who are new to the sport to give it a try! It would be great to see more families at Paddlefest, for example, and more people trying a kayak or canoe for the first time.

Well, we didn't bring a new paddler with us this time, but we certainly had a good time anyway. I enjoyed looking at the maps of the Salish Sea, especially the map for the Georgia Strait Community Alliance with annotations useful for small boaters. There were a couple of raffles to enter. It's good policy to enter raffles, especially when they're fundraising for good causes.

We made a tour of all the booths, even though several were closed, and checked out the kayaks on display. I got my hands on a Greenland paddle that had been made for someone about my size – small grip, short stature. (There don't seem to be any paddles meant for plump and slow people, though, darn it.)

So far, every time we attend Paddlefest, someone from our paddle group wins a door prize or other great swag. This year Bernie won a bag with a t-shirt, a ball cap, small stuff sack and a travel mug!

And when we got back to the Beach House after touring some other neat-o places, we got a phone call from Cheryl of Sealegs Kayaking Adventures. Turns out, we won the raffle's first prize – a Mini Tripper kids kayak from Jackson Kayak!

So, we're heading back up to Ladysmith someday soon to pick it up... oh joy!

WHAT WE PASS BY EVERY Day

There are everyday miracles and wonders all around us much of the time. There are wonders to be found even in cities where the marks of feet trampling the ground tend to obscure the unique elements of a place until it seems that everything is the colour and shape of footprints. One of the ways we see these wonders is to get into our kayaks and visit urban waterways. Some of these places have made us crow with delight. I'm thinking in particular of days spent paddling on the Humber River in Toronto and the New Credit River in Mississauga and Toronto Islands where one is never really out of sight of the city.

Then there are also days we paddle on the Gorge, along the suburban shores and up the little streams where in some places the parkland is so lush that it's hard to remember we're right in the middle of a city, not on its edges. Or days we paddle at Discovery and Chatham Islands, where in places it's impossible to believe we're not in a wondrously isolated wilderness, but really only a mile from Oak Bay's tearooms.

Now I'm reminded that there are everyday miracles and wonders to be found in most places. Take Drumheller, Alberta, for example. It was the end point for my kayaking trip on the Red Deer River. I've walked through much of Drumheller on a few visits, and can report that there's a layer of amber-coloured dust over almost everything in town. The marks of footprints are everywhere that isn't paved. And in one well-trampled part of town, what looked like a bumpy rock turned out to be a dinosaur skull.

To be fair, after fossilization it was also a bumpy rock. In a playground. How many dinosaur fossil fans have trodden on this big ol' fossil in recent years? No one knows. I figure this is a lesson to us all, to be aware of wonders and miracles underfoot and all around us. Instead of dividing the world into "Exciting Places" and "Oh Well – Dull Old Home" let's be ready to keep urban paddling part of our expeditions, and practise our rockhound skills at home as well as in the field in distant places.

HAD A GOOD TIME ON the water on Saturday. Bernie and I launched at Cooper's Cove and headed into Hutchison Cove. Both coves are part of Sooke Basin, where we've paddled before several times.

We ate a ripe blackberry each as we walked from the van to shore with our boats. No lingering to harvest blackberries! Today was just a short day. If I'd thought about driving to water, I'd have taken my 13-foot Expedition inflatable kayak, but the little 8'6" Lagoon is still so new that I'm practically carrying it to the grocery store and everywhere. I was in the Lagoon and Bernie in the red Pamlico when we set off. By the time I hit the water – a bare six minutes after leaving the van, I might add, which is a terrific inflation/set-up time for any folding kayak – my spouse was drifting back from the middle of the cove with a smug smile.

"I've already caught a crab," he said. "And a fish. Well, the fish struck at the blackberry seed I spit out of my teeth. And I've seen a turkey vulture soaring overhead. My day is complete." Congratulations were in order, even when he admitted that the crab had been thumb-sized, floating, and already released, and the fish was a tiny fingerling.

Most of the sea life we noted after that was a series of jellyfish. Moon jellies were floating all around. We paddled past the bluffs and into the mouth of Hutchison Cove, where we drifted for a while and contemplated an immensely large house visible on the shore.

We followed along the Goodridge Peninsula on the outside of Cooper Cove and then on the inside, contemplating the geology and the wear-and-tear on this little peninsula. It formed after the end of the last Ice Age, and most of the sediments we can see above the waterline piled up in the last 10,000 years. There are clamshells and black earth here, which apparently means the ashes and shells from First Nations middens. It would have been a nice place for clams and ducks. A hundred years ago it was a site for construction of concrete tunnel sections to convey water from Sooke Lake reservoir to Victoria, so the site saw some pretty rough use. Now it's recovering and looks like a park. Part of the Cove is a sanctuary for migrating birds.

A seal or two popped up behind our boats and watched us before dipping down again. We weren't on the water long, but it always feels like the right place to be.

Don't miss out!

Visit the website below and you can sign up to receive emails whenever Paula Johanson publishes a new book. There's no charge and no obligation.

https://books2read.com/r/B-A-ZKUK-HLTOB

BOOKS 2 READ

Connecting independent readers to independent writers.

Did you love *Green Paddler*? Then you should read *King Kwong: Larry Kwong, the China Clipper Who Broke the NHL Colour Barrier*[1] by Paula Johanson!

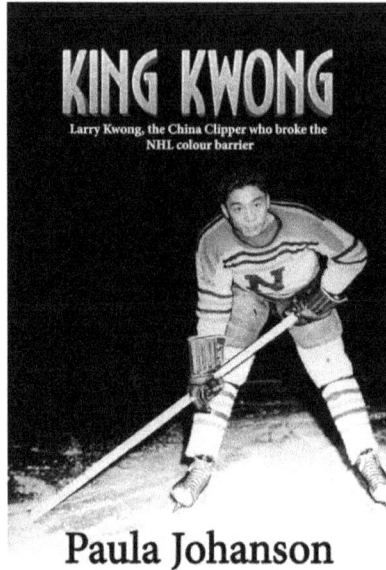

Paula Johanson

[2]

Who broke the colour barrier in the NHL? A man whose professional hockey career statistics include leading the senior leagues for scoring and for low penalty minutes -- and a single shift on the ice in an NHL game. He was scouted three times by NHL teams before that game, and courted away from the NHL to a powerful role in three different international leagues before retiring.

He is Larry Kwong, a Canadian of Chinese heritage born in Vernon BC in 1923, a hard-working man and World War II serviceman who played hockey most of his life.

Author Paula Johanson explores the life and accomplishments of the China Clipper, Larry Kwong. His story is one of an indomitable spirit who triumphs

---

1. https://books2read.com/u/bOX6oA

2. https://books2read.com/u/bOX6oA

in the face of adversity and social discrimination. In 2013, Kwong was inducted into the BC Sports Hall of Fame as a pioneer.

"If you're not familiar with Larry Kwong, prepare to be amazed. This game-changing hero should be a household name in Canada and the hockey world. His inspiring story is one for the ages, yet it's still not widely known.

Author Paula Johanson brings justice to Kwong's extraordinary life. All the elements of classic fiction are here, and yet this is riveting history. We follow the ultimate long shot as he chases the 'impossible'...and triggers a shift in his society.

Johanson retraces Kwong's trailblazing strides with dexterity and grace. It's a mythic journey. From underclass underdog, he emerges as a larger-than-life hero. Transported, we can cheer on King Kwong as he smashes stereotypes and barriers with uncommon skill and class.

This is a long-overdue but timeless biography—a spellbinding tale of a puck magician whose escape from opposition checks and societal chains helped to recast a fairer future for us all."

- Chad Soon, Director, Greater Vernon Museum & Archives and Okanagan Sports Hall of Fame.

Doublejoy Books is pleased to present this fine biography, *King Kwong*, previously released by Five Rivers Publishing. This new edition includes an afterword by Chad Soon.

Read more at books2read.com/paulaj.

Also by Paula Johanson

Prime Ministers of Canada
Pierre Elliott Trudeau: Child of Nature
Charles Tupper: Warhorse

Young Science
Bat Poop Sparkles

Standalone
Small Rain and Other Nightmares
Island Views
Plum Tree
Tower in the Crooked Wood
King Kwong: Larry Kwong, the China Clipper Who Broke the NHL Colour
Barrier
Woolgathering: Awareness of the Foreign in Published Works About
Cowichan Woolworking
Science Critters
Green Paddler

Watch for more at books2read.com/paulaj.

About the Author

Paula Johanson is a Canadian writer. A graduate of the University of Victoria with an MA in Canadian literature, she has worked as a security guard, a short order cook, a teacher, newspaper writer, and more. As well as editing books and teaching materials, she has run an organic-method small farm with her spouse, raised gifted twins, and cleaned university dormitories. In addition to novels and stories, she is the author of forty-two books written for educational publishers, among them *The Paleolithic Revolution* and *Women Writers* from the series *Defying Convention: Women Who Changed The World*. Johanson is an active member of SF Canada, the national association of science fiction and fantasy authors.

Read more at books2read.com/paulaj.

DOUBLEJOY BOOKS

About the Publisher

Doublejoy Books is the publisher of a variety of eclectic books of Canadian literature.

http://doublejoybooks.com
http://books2read.com/paulaj

www.ingramcontent.com/pod-product-compliance
Lightning Source LLC
Chambersburg PA
CBHW032142040426
42449CB00005B/369